Life Economics

Time • Space • Interpersonal Relationships

Shih Cheng Yen

人生經濟學【英文版】

人生經濟學

作　　者：釋證嚴

翻　　譯：美國總會文發室翻譯團隊

編 輯 群：美國總會文發室文編組

美術設計：美國總會文發室媒體布展組

出 版 者：靜思人文志業股份有限公司

出版日期：2013年3月

Life Economics

Author : Shih Cheng Yen

Translation Team : Translation Team of the Tzu Chi USA

Editorial Team : Editing Division, Humanistic Culture
Development Department, Tzu Chi USA

Graphic Design : Multimedia Design Division, Humanistic
Culture Development Department, Tzu Chi USA

Publisher : Jing Si Publications

First Print : March 2013

Jing Si Publications, Taiwan
ISBN:978-986-6661-43-3

www.tzuchi.org

Contents

Preface

As we look around our world, we can see that natural disasters have become more and more common in recent years: blizzards in China, floods in South America, forest fires in the United States, and typhoons in Southeast Asia have all caused countless casualties. As the greenhouse effect leads to global warming, scientists predict that climate change will make our weather ever more extreme.

The state of the earth's ecology is truly very worrisome. If we wish to mitigate this ecological crisis, we must first purify our minds. We must all unite and work together to help those who suffer. We must seize the opportunity to make good use of time and space, and inspire others to do good.

In Buddhism, we think of time in three stages: past, present, and future, or yesterday, today, and tomorrow. Time has neither beginning nor end. Even what we think of as the past has more past before it. How do we seize the present and the limitless future?

Good and bad karma both accumulate over time, and the slightest deviation in trajectory can lead one far astray. Even though human beings are puny and fragile on the grand scale of the universe, if we confuse happiness with indulgence in a lavish lifestyle, then all the miniscule bad karmas we accumulate eventually pile into a significant burden of bad karma. Just as the mighty redwood is no match for the countless termites that gnaw at it day and night, even the strongest person cannot withstand the invasion of bacteria. So it is with Earth: despite its enormous size, it cannot endure the destruction caused by all sentient beings.

We should make good use of our time to benefit others. With today's advanced technology, we are connected to the entire world while remaining here in Taiwan. We cannot begrudge our time, stress only our own needs, and care only for our immediate surroundings. Rather, we should be concerned with world affairs and the well-being of all sentient beings.

Space is the environment we inhabit. The Earth on which we live is the common home of all sentient beings. We must broaden our minds and step out from our personal spaces to help and care for one another.

Tzu Chi has always upheld a humanitarian spirit of great love that transcends nationality and race. That is why Tzu Chi today enjoys such a broad base of support. Whenever there is suffering, help arrives from all directions. This is what it means to broaden the space of our love. Choose the right direction and seize every moment to accumulate good karma and blessings. Steadily extend kindness and expand great love with each step. When we utilize time and space to the fullest, we will have a positive outlook on life.

Nature continually presents new challenges to humanity. In the tug-of-war between good and evil, each individual's power is limited and a small group has only meager strength. To face these challenges, everyone must work together in unison. With strength in numbers, blessings will flourish. To achieve this, we must create good affinities with others and give diligently.

Each person who cultivates a benevolent heart is planting a seed. If we diligently nurture these seeds of goodness, they will sprout and flourish. Over time, seeds of love will continue to grow and multiply forever.

If we use our time to do good deeds and positively influence one another through our interactions, then the selfless love in our hearts will spread. This will encourage people to join hands and hearts and purify their minds. Therefore, we must give more of ourselves so that disasters in the world will cease and peace and harmony will come to all.

Jing Si Abode
Hualien, Taiwan
November 2009

Part One — **Time**

There are good times and bad times, and ups and downs to the world economy.

In our lives, time passed can never be retrieved.

Therefore, we should pay attention to the "time economy" in our lives.

Chapter 1 - Time through a Microscope

Time often troubles us. It has no substance to be caught or held. It has no form or figure to be seen. It is always coming and going around us.

Our perception of time is limited to people and events. But in reality time is like the shifting sands of an endless river accumulating into the infinite future. Before today, lay the boundless past. According to scientists, the Earth is 4.6 billion years old. Compared to the lifespan of the human race, this is indeed a long time, and it does not even include the immeasurable time that passed before the Earth came into existence.

In Buddhism, we say that there are three periods of time: present, past, and future. Today's past is yesterday; its future is tomorrow. Yesterday also has its past, which is day before yesterday. Similarly, up to the moment of our birth, we have had many previous lives. Does life have a limit? No. Because each past has its own past, there are countless pasts. The river of time has brought us to this life, this moment.

Will there be a future after today? Will our future end in the next moment? Or tomorrow? No one knows.

Section 1 – The Clock that Cannot Be Turned Back

Although a clock shows the same time today as it did yesterday, the day is not the same. When we say "now" at this instant, it has become the "past" as soon as we have said it. So how can it still be "now"? Time keeps slipping away without pause. This is the law of emptiness.

Our life is like a clock. But when a clock runs too fast, we can slow it down; yet we can never turn back the clock of life. So we should cherish every second and not procrastinate or waste time.

● The Equality of Time

In this world, people appear to differ in wealth and status, but in reality, all are truly equal. For instance, each person has the same twenty-four hours every day. It all depends on how each individual uses these hours.

A wise person considers only the time spent in working and contributing as using time. Each day, from the moment our eyes open and our consciousness stirs until we rest at night, we interact with the surrounding environment. This period of time is useable time. Therefore, if we do not get up at six o'clock, but keep sleeping until eight, those two hours would be wasted.

We cannot save extra hours for tomorrow by sleeping earlier today. The reservoir of time is emptied each day, just like a computer is wiped clean of its files. Each day, time starts anew. It is the same for everybody, whether rich or poor, noble or lowborn. All have the same twenty-four hours, not a second more.

We have the right to use time while awake, but not while asleep: a law that applies to all. The important thing is how we use it. As time goes by, we all produce different karmic seeds. Good or bad, they are all "saved in the file." So we must use our time well for good karma to accumulate.

Some people do neither evil nor good, but simply spend each day in pleasure. Their lives are wasted. We should seize every moment to do good deeds and plant seeds of goodness. Wasting time is like shortening our lifespan.

In the reservoir of life, time is limited. Each morning as we open our eyes, we should realize that there is only so much time. Time unused is time wasted. Not only should we make good use of each day, we should also seize every moment to do good deeds and accumulate merit. Moreover, we must be very careful in our actions. For instance, when we see an old woman fall down, we should quickly reach out to help her up and show our care by asking, "Are you alright?" This is an act of kindness. The old woman will say, "Thank you. You are a good person." This is an act of virtue. We accumulate good deeds and merits if we always give rise to good thoughts and take actions accordingly. This is how we avoid wasting the time we have.

● **Losing One Year of Age per Year**

Samantabhadra's Verse of Admonition says, "The day has passed, and life has shortened with it. Just as a fish in a drying pond, what joy is there?" When I get up each day, I ask myself what has to be done today. In the evening, as the day comes to an end, I reflect on whether I have finished everything I meant to do. I feel that once the day has passed my life is one day shorter, just like the fish in a tank whose water is diminishing drop by drop. As we approach the end of our lives, we can perish at any time, like fish without water.

At the beginning of each new year, when people say "Happy New Year," I cannot help but think, "Another year has passed; what's so happy about that?" Some would say, "Because we're one year older." I actually think of it as "one year less." If one can live to be eighty, then with each passing year, does he not have one less year to live? So "one year older" is actually "one year less" in our life.

Whenever I think of this, I wonder why we toil through life fussing over trivial things. We busy ourselves with work and compete with others openly or in secret; yet when we pass away, we can take nothing with us except our karma. Good or bad, whether we want it or not, each of us must take with us all the karma accumulated throughout our lives. Therefore, there is nothing in life worth fussing over except time. We must cherish the time we have and use it to the fullest.

Although working nonstop is tiresome, when you look at it from another perspective, feeling tired or not is simply a matter of attitude. For example, sometimes I feel physically exhausted, too. But whenever I think about taking a break, another thought comes to my mind: "Idling away one hour is letting one hour of life slip away. I cannot let it pass in vain. I have to make it fruitful." This is how you can change your perspective.

We often say that it is a blessing to be healthy and a blessing to be able to work. With this understanding, we will not waste time. Once there was a volunteer who was being treated for cancer in Tzu Chi Hospital's Heart Lotus Ward (See note). She posted a note on her headboard: "If you love me, please do not ask me to sleep." She knew she was in the terminal stage of her disease, so she wanted to do as much volunteer work as possible. Everyone was concerned about her condition and always wanted her to rest. So she wrote that note asking people to let her make best use of the time she had left. Why rest? If something is right, we should seize every moment to do it.

At the beginning of each new year, everyone fills in new calendars and makes new resolutions, hoping that each day we may reach our goals, fulfill our wishes, and do things that make us happy and at ease. We all hope that we can complete each page full of plans, and adjust our life direction. However, we soon become too busy or tired, and let go of our original plans.

Whether or not our plans are carried out, time does not stop ticking, and life keeps slipping away.

(Note – The Heart Lotus Ward is the hospice facility in Tzu Chi General Hospital where medical professionals, social workers, volunteers, and religious personnel provide services to terminally ill patients and their families. These include medical services as well as physical and spiritual care and guidance.)

● **Time Keeps Ticking Away**

Nothing tangible on earth can stand still. The earth turns, giving us four seasons each year as well as light and darkness each day. But we hardly notice that the earth is revolving. It is the same with the human body. When did our hair grow long? Every so often we need to cut our nails again; at which second, which minute, or on which day did they grow long? We have no idea at all. New cells are born as old ones perish. Starting as a baby, we become a teenager, then enter into adulthood and old age. The whole process takes place without us knowing it.

I remember one day thirty years ago a mother brought her little girl to the Jing Si Abode. This girl had just started kindergarten. She was hungry, so her mother gave her a bottle of milk.

While lying there drinking milk, she asked, "Mama, can I not grow up?"

Her mother asked, "Why?"

She said, "Since I'm little, I can lie down and drink milk, right?"

Her mother replied, "Right. Drink up so you can grow up big and strong."

The girl said, "I don't want to grow up, so I can always lie down and drink milk like this."

I was deeply impressed by this dialogue. When I saw her again a few years ago, she had grown from a little girl into a young woman. Everyone has only one childhood. Every day comes but once. When time passes it will never come back again. Once something has happened, it is hard to make amends. Objects may be reproduced, but a fracture in time or in the heart is impossible to mend.

Our lives are truly very short. They last only a few decades. Therefore we must constantly remind ourselves that as long as the direction is correct, we should seize the moment and do what is right. Otherwise, if we miss an opportunity, it will never come back. We only live once; "once" means each life experience happens only one time.

A group of students once asked Socrates how they may experience truth. He told them, "I'll show you through an experiment." Socrates brought them to an orchard and said, "Walk from the entrance all the way through to the exit. You may choose any fruit along the way. However, you must choose the best, the most beautiful, the one you like the most. You may only pick one, and you cannot go back." The students entered the orchard. Seeing the trees full of fruit, they could not decide which one was the best and the most beautiful. Before they knew it, they came to the end of the orchard. Socrates then asked them, "Have you picked the best and the most beautiful fruit?"

"Master, please give us another chance," they pleaded.

"Why haven't you picked any fruit?" Socrates asked.

One student replied, "When I first entered the orchard, I saw a very large and pretty fruit, but I thought maybe there were bigger and better ones inside. I was worried that if I picked the first one, I would have no chance to pick a better one later."

The master said, "This is the great truth: we only have one chance in life. We are only young once, too. We can never go back."

People often say, "If I had known better, I never would have done it." We must set our life's goals and purposes in the right direction. No matter how far it is or how much time it takes to get there, we must walk on earnestly. If we have the mentality that "I can do it tomorrow if I can't get it done today," then we do not lead an earnest life.

Section 2 – Will Tomorrow Come for Sure?

On September 21, 1999, at 1:47am, the earth suddenly shook violently in Taiwan; it was the devastating 921 Earthquake. At that time some people had not gone to bed yet. They might have been planning the next day's business, full of hope for tomorrow. Some might have already been asleep, dreaming sweet dreams. Others might have been quarreling and wanting to separate from each other the following day. There were many different life dramas.

No matter what their plans had been, when the earthquake hit, sweet dreams were shattered in an instant: the friends they planned to meet might have been gone forever; the people they wanted to separate from could have passed away in the earthquake; the survivors grieved with agonizing pain. Life is truly impermanent.

● Will We Live to See Tomorrow?

Everything we do, we must do with diligence and perseverance. In the case of spiritual cultivation, we may practice diligently in the beginning, but as time goes by, we can easily become mindless in our daily lives. Sluggishness and mindlessness are the two major forces that stop our wisdom-life from growing.

There is a story about King Yama, the ruler of hell. One day, King Yama realized that fewer and fewer people were being banished to hell. He expressed his concern to the ghost soldiers, asking, "What should be done to boost our population?"

General Ox-head replied, "I can go to the human realm and tell people that there is no heaven and therefore no need to do good deeds. No matter how many good deeds they do or how many good intentions they have, they are all useless."

King Yama shook his head and said, "This will not be forceful enough."

General Horse-face said, "I can go tell the humans that there is no hell so they can do whatever they want."

King Yama did not think this would be effective, either. Then, a little ghost spoke up, "I can tell the humans that there's always tomorrow."

King Yama was very pleased with the idea and said, "Yes! You go and tell the humans that there will always be tomorrow for everyone. It is human nature to become sluggish. If people know that tomorrow awaits them, they will think they still have time. Spiritual cultivation? They can do it tomorrow. Good deeds? They have tomorrow to do it. They will put all their hopes on tomorrow. As a result, their determination and diligence will dissolve. They will become sluggish and ultimately fall into hell."

From this story we can see that life is impermanent. How can we still hold expectation for tomorrow?

On December 26, 2004, a massive earthquake hit near Aceh, Indonesia, and triggered a tsunami that swept over more than ten countries in South and Southeast Asia. Within minutes, over 50,000 people were killed in Sri Lanka and more than 240,000 people lost their lives in Banda Aceh, Indonesia. The total number of casualties in the region remains unknown. It all happened in an instant. Life is truly impermanent.

The tsunami wiped out numerous buildings with its destructive force. One convenience store had just celebrated its grand opening at nine o'clock that morning. Shortly after nine it was swept away. A ship taller than a three-story building stood in front of a half-destroyed building. It had been pushed six kilometers from the sea to land on a street.

A time of crisis is also a time for great awakening. Witnessing that life is impermanent, that our homeland is fragile, and life or death is determined in an instant, do we truly know whether we will live to see tomorrow? What are we still fussing over in life? The important thing is to stay positive and do what needs to be done when it is right and we are still able to do it. We must also bring forth the love in our hearts and make this love last. After the tsunami, the sea became calm and beautiful once more. When will the turbid waves of our society become pure and clean again?

There are 365 days in a year, 3,650 days in a decade. Many people think that even if today is wasted, there is still tomorrow. If tomorrow is wasted, many more days remain in the year. If the whole year is idled away, we still have thousands of days left in the decade. We think our life is infinite, so we tend to waste it. We really need to remind ourselves that life is impermanent.

Although we are safe and sound today, we don't know what tomorrow will bring. Being happy now, we don't know what will happen next. Therefore, we must always seize each moment to do good deeds. If we only daydream, our life is empty and useless.

What constitutes a happy life? To really feel grounded and stable, that will be a happy life.

● Life Exists Between Breaths

When I wake up each morning, I stretch my arms and move my legs. If I can move freely, turn over and sit up, I feel grateful. One should feel content at having a clear mind and being healthy. Can we foresee that we will live through the next twenty-four hours safely? It is difficult to say.

One day the Buddha addressed his followers, "My dear disciples, you have followed me in spiritual cultivation for so long; do you know the true meaning of life yet?"

The followers looked at one another, wondering what the answer could be. Then one disciple volunteered an answer: "Life exists from day to day."

The Buddha shook his head and said, "You still do not know the truth of life."

Another disciple then offered, "Life exists from meal to meal."

The Buddha shook his head again.

Then a disciple said, "Life exists from one breath to the next."

The Buddha smiled. "Right; life exists between breaths."

When we can exhale and inhale smoothly, we are alive. We often think little of breathing, believing that it is a simple matter. However, our life exists between breaths.

Mr. Feng and his wife have been Tzu Chi volunteers for over ten years. His father is very amiable, and has joined Tzu Chi as a recycling volunteer after retirement. The Feng family is full of diligent Tzu Chi volunteers.

I remember visiting Buddhist Tzu Chi General Hospital in Xindian one day. Afterwards, I went to check on the crops at the Da Ai Farm adjacent to the hospital. Then I stopped by the recycling station, which was very clean and tidy. The elder Mr. Feng chatted with me cheerfully, and expressed his gratitude at having the recycling center to work happily in.

He cherished his ability to work, and although retired, he never stopped working. One day, he suddenly felt tightness in his chest. He looked fine on the outside, but since the recycling center is close to the hospital, he decided to walk there to see a doctor.

The outpatient physician suggested that he first take an electrocardiogram. Since the electrocardiogram room was only one floor up, he did not take the elevator. On the landing of the staircase he suddenly toppled over. Because few people used the stairs, he was not found until ten minutes later. Due to the delayed rescue, he had to stay in intensive care for some time.

According to the elder Mrs. Feng, the clearest sentence Mr. Feng uttered after he got out of intensive care was: "Do recycling well. Dispatch two more trucks. Stack things well." After that he never said another word. He was subsequently transferred to a nursing home.

The younger Mr. Feng is a filial son. He continues the recycling work and visits his father in the nursing home every day. He often tells his father, "The Master says that whatever is meant to happen will happen, so we should accept it gladly when it comes." The elder Mrs. Feng never once complained. She often speaks to her husband, too.

The younger Mr. Feng once said, "My father didn't waste his life. He kept working until the moment he fell down." The entire family exemplifies understanding, tolerance, faith, and selfless love. The Fengs understand the law of cause and effect. They also understand karmic retribution. I am truly grateful for and touched by them. The law of nature is that all things come and go, without any warning at times. We don't know when the end will come. Therefore, we must cherish life and understand how to seize each moment.

● We Cannot Wait

Time never stops. We must cherish each day and make the best use of time to do good deeds. If we do not take hold of time, it will be like starting to dig a well when we feel thirsty or trying to fix a leak when the boat is already in midstream. It will be too late.

People often say, "Spiritual cultivation? I will do that when I'm old," or, "What I cannot accomplish today, I'll start tomorrow!" It is as if we have plenty of time tomorrow. In reality, tomorrow is another day. We have other things to do tomorrow. When today has passed, it is gone forever. Do not keep waiting and pushing back time.

Some people think they possess plenty of time because they are young. Others think they can rely on their wealth and power. But when the end comes, whether faced with failing health or impending death, everyone is helpless. No matter how much money you have, money cannot buy time.

I always feel that time is running out. Like a spool of thread on a sewing machine, when the spool is full it does not seem to turn very fast, but when the thread is almost used up, the spool seems to turn faster and faster as the foot pedal is pressed. When we are young, we hardly notice time's passing, as if we still have lots of time. If we cannot finish a task in this hour, we still have the next hour or two to do it. However, as we age we begin to realize that every day passes quickly and time indeed waits for no one.

Life diminishes as time goes by. People should help one another in a timely manner. Even if another person needs only a little, if we can give assistance in time, he will be very grateful. But if someone is in need and we are unwilling to give, hoping to wait until after we have saved enough for ourselves, that is not helping in a timely manner. No matter how great our wealth, it will be worthless.

The ancient Chinese philosopher Zhuangzi was once too poor to buy food, so he asked his friend to lend him three liters of millet. The friend told him, "I don't have too much right now, but I'll lend you three hundred taels of gold once I collect taxes from the villagers."

Upon hearing this, Zhuangzi sighed and said, "On my way here I saw a tiny puddle about to dry out. A fish in the puddle called out to me to bring it a few glasses of water. I told the fish, 'Let me go to the kingdoms of Wu and Yue and ask the kings' permission to channel water here from their rivers. Then I can return you to the ocean.' The fish became very angry and said, 'Then you might as well visit the fishmonger tomorrow to find me as a dried fish!'" Having said this to his friend, Zhuangzi left.

What the impoverished Zhuangzi needed was only three liters of millet. To him, three hundred taels of gold was unimaginable and not what he needed. Those in need do not ask for much. Yet those who are well-off are either too stingy or worried that they will lose face if they give too little that they miss the opportunity to help others in time.

Life is impermanent. We cannot control what we will achieve in the future. Many years ago a man shared this story with me. He told me that a friend of his was well-to-do but lived frugally. Though he had much, he hardly ever thought about others' deficiency.

This man often told his rich friend to do some good deeds, but his friend always replied, "I will when I have made enough money."

But when would that be? Nobody knows. One day at meal time this friend suddenly lowered his head and lost consciousness. He was taken to an emergency room.

Therefore, we cannot wait until we have enough. We cannot wait until we are wealthy to do good deeds, especially when we cannot be sure that we will be rich in the future. After Taiwan's devastating 921 Earthquake in 1999, Tzu Chi determined to rebuild fifty schools in the Project Hope program. Why were we so bold at that time? We did not have abundant funding then, but we had a sense of urgency. Why? The schools were damaged or destroyed; the students could not wait. Elementary school has only six years and middle school only three. If schools cannot resume quickly, how could the students receive a proper education? How could they study with peace of mind in makeshift tents?

We often need to seize the opportunity and take immediate action. We successfully rebuilt fifty schools in two years, even though we had no money at first. After making the commitment to restore the schools, we then inspired people to donate their resources and labor. I am grateful to the Tzu Chi volunteers in Taiwan and worldwide for their efforts to make Project Hope a great success. Thinking back, I was indeed audacious then. But fortunately I made the decision in time, otherwise how could we have rebuilt those schools?

We must not wait until conditions are perfect before we do something. Each person much chose his or her own path in life. If this path is pointed in the right direction, then we must seize the opportunity and take action. It is the same with contributing to society. Some excuse themselves by saying they are too young, that they will contribute when they are older and have fewer obligations. But how long can they wait before they have free time? Finding time wisely in a busy schedule to do good deeds is definitely the right thing to do.

Section Three – Life's Treasure Trove

Time is a rare treasure in our lives. From birth, our lives are inextricably intertwined with time. With time, we grow up, finish schooling, and make a name for ourselves. But it is also the accumulation of time that causes human beings to age and all things to perish. While time accomplishes all, it also destroys all. Therefore, we should cherish and make good use of time. We must embrace every second to do good deeds and develop wisdom, accumulate virtue, and build compassion.

I often *say blessing is experiencing joy through action; wisdom is gaining spiritual freedom through understanding.* What gives us joy? The answer is doing good deeds. If we fight with others and fuss over trivial matters, we end up wasting time and hurting others, but not benefiting ourselves. Wisdom is to be able to utilize time for good, and as a result feel at ease and worry free.

● Everything Can Be Achieved With Time

In this world, nothing is more merciless than time. Yet nothing is more lovable than time, because time can achieve everything.

There was once a king who had a baby girl. He adored his daughter very much and wished that she would grow up quickly.

The more he anticipated her growth, the slower it felt. Seeing his daughter still so small every day, the king posted a proclamation asking, "Who can make my daughter grow up fast?" After a period of time, a wise elder saw the proclamation, tore it off the wall, and requested to see the king.

The king asked, "Are you confident that you can speed up my daughter's growth?"

The elder replied, "Yes, but you must give me time."

The king was delighted, "As long as you can make my daughter grow up, I will grant you anything you desire."

The elder said, "Then, please give me sixteen years."

The king agreed.

"But during this period of time," the elder continued, "you may not see your daughter. Is that agreeable?"

Again, the king nodded.

Sixteen years later, the elder brought the girl before the king as he had promised. Seeing his daughter, the king exclaimed happily, "Amazing! You have turned my little girl into a beautiful princess."

The king thought the elder was brilliant. He failed to see that it is the law of nature for children to grow up with time.

Both success and failure in life are accumulated with time. A person who knows how to make good use of time will live life to its fullest. One who squanders time, on the other hand, will have an empty and meaningless existence. If we walk deliberately and steadfastly down the road of life, we will be able to look back with a warm feeling, knowing that our life was worthwhile. Having learned this, it is never too late to start making good use of time. But if we continue to waste time, it will definitely be too late.

When in school, we must take hold of time to study wholeheartedly, pay full attention in class, and accumulate academic achievements. This is time's accumulation of academic success. It is the same with business: if one can take hold of time to manage a business attentively, he will achieve business success through time. Likewise, in spiritual cultivation, we must seize every moment to practice towards enlightenment.

Time can also make us feel completely helpless. The joyful moments of yesterday have passed, and we cannot hold onto them forever. We cannot undo a regretful action, either. Therefore, we must be mindful of our actions and not accumulate regrets or wrongdoings because of sheer carelessness. If we continue to have bad relationships with others, it will eventually become bad karma.

On the other hand, if we work diligently to cleanse our mind, make good vows, speak good words, and do good deeds to please others, others will be touched by our behavior. As a result, everybody will be at ease. This is how to accumulate blessings and live a life with no regrets. *Never pass up a good deed because it is minor; never commit an evil deed because it is minuscule.* Do not think that you are a virtuous person with only some bad habitual tendencies. Think about it: Don't all villains become the way they are because they have accumulated many bad habitual tendencies? Good and evil arise at each thought. We certainly cannot take this lightly.

We should utilize our time to serve others, and in giving, observe, feel, and analyze life. As we learn to differentiate tangible matters from the abstract principles of existence, and use our wisdom to comprehend everything, we can achieve excellence in academics, business, and our mission in life. We can then help and inspire ourselves as well as others, and become truly wise people.

● Never-ending Homework

Time is fleeting; time wasted is an equal amount of life shortened. We have been given the gift of life; we must not slack off or succumb to laziness. If we actively serve others when we are physically and mentally healthy, we will create good affinities with others every day. Some people live their lives in earnest, devoting themselves to benefiting the public. Even after they have passed away, their spirits live on. These are truly lives of value!

Life includes the physical body as well as the spiritual wisdom-life. We cannot keep our bodies forever. As life goes on we cannot maintain our youthful energy and good looks, nor can we stop the process of aging. What is the point of cherishing the physical shell of our body? The Buddha teaches us to value our wisdom-life. Wisdom-life has no distinction of age or beauty, nor will it change its form. It can exist eternally in the universe.

"Wisdom-life" is attained when we, with our physical bodies, join others in our intention to give willingly. In doing so, everyone's wisdom-life will grow.

Both blessing and wisdom are accumulated in daily living. I once read a book about a Buddhist practitioner's method of spiritual cultivation. This practitioner lived in a monastery deep in the mountains. Each day he went out to sit on a rock protruding from the edge of a cliff. With half of it hanging in the air, the rock would sway slightly whenever the wind blew. Therefore, the practitioner had to sit with great caution. Facing the danger of falling off the cliff was his way to tame his mind.

In the beginning he was terrified, but he made up his mind to obtain enlightenment from the tranquility of nature. So, even when gusts of wind set the rock wobbling, he was determined to maintain a disciplined and calm mind. He certainly could not doze off and allow his body to topple over and fall down the cliff. He had no choice but to train himself in steadiness, endurance, and prudence.

One day the practitioner got tired. He closed his eyes and drifted off to sleep. All of a sudden he felt the rock falling. At the critical moment, he felt protective deities hold him up. He woke up and was very pleased with himself, because he had trained so well that the protective deities were with him. So he relaxed and continued to sit. Soon he started to nod off again. At that moment he heard the deities scold him harshly, "You only get one chance, not a second, and certainly not a third!"

This story tells us that we should always be vigilant. Only through self-realization, self-awareness, and experiencing the truth with our lives can we develop our wisdom-life.

Although life is impermanent and brief, we should not view our life so lightly that we readily exchange it for wisdom-life. I read a story about a big church in Philadelphia that had been a small chapel a century ago. A little girl of six or seven was sobbing outside of the chapel one day. The pastor walked up to the girl and asked, "Why are you crying here?"

The little girl replied, "It is too crowded, I can't get in." The church was packed with people and she could not squeeze in to attend Sunday school. The girl was heartbroken.

Seeing her shabby clothes, the pastor figured that she was from a nearby slum. He took her into the church and found her a seat to sit down. From then on, she never missed a day of Sunday school.

Two years later the little girl became ill and unexpectedly passed away. Her parents knew their daughter was a devout believer, so they called for the pastor. As he mournfully held the girl in his arms, a worn purse dropped out. A note in the purse had these words scribbled on it: "I am grateful to be able to attend Sunday school. But the chapel is too small and many people cannot come in. I wish to turn this small chapel into a big church."

The girl had started to save every penny she had, and the pastor found fifty-seven cents in her small purse. Seeing her savings and her wish, the pastor was moved to tears. He wanted to help the little girl fulfill her wish. But since most of the families in the parish were poor, the fundraising went on slowly little by little.

One day this heart-wrenching story was reported by the local newspaper. A prominent landowner told the pastor, "I have a piece of land for sale."

The pastor replied that he had no money to buy it.

The landowner said, "Yes, you do. I want to sell this piece of land to you for fifty-seven cents." The pastor purchased the land with the young girl's money, and the local residents also donated fervently to the worthy cause. The small chapel eventually became a large church that could accommodate three thousand and three hundred people.

This little girl died young, but left behind a small wish that inspired a monumental project. Her story still touches people's hearts after a hundred years. Isn't this eternal wisdom-life?

Chapter 2 - Time Flies; Time Crawls

When we cannot let go of the things troubling our minds, we feel that time passes slowly and unbearably. But when we are happy and joyful, time seems to pass quickly. Therefore, we should train ourselves to maintain a healthy and positive attitude in our daily lives. This kind of attitude will help us deal with undesirable situations. Even when we are facing unavoidable illness, the pain will pass quickly if we accept the illness with gratitude and respect towards life.

Time is ticking away. If we can make the best use of every second while stepping firmly and steadily forward, then we will be able to accomplish much every day. On the other hand, if we do not take good care of our minds, we may succumb to incorrect thoughts and lose our direction at any moment. As a result, negative karma will be created and we may be born as lower creatures in our next life. It is said that once you lose your human form, it will take eons to be reborn as human again.

Section 1 – Diamond or Dirt?

Life is short. It lasts only a few decades. Why then do we hurry through life? What's the rush? Are we moving toward suffering and karmic obstructions, or moving toward a bright realm filled with love and vigor?

Time treats everyone equally, yet each individual's feeling about time is different. It all depends on how we use each moment, starting from the time we open our eyes in the early morning. When we make good use of each moment positively and happily, we become living Bodhisattvas. When we use time inappropriately, however, we may destroy our beautiful earth, and do harm to others as well as to ourselves.

● Spend Time Where It Counts

I often say that a wise man treats time like diamonds while a fool treats time like dirt. In general, diamonds are considered precious and valuable, so they are a metaphor for value and importance. But the value of diamonds cannot really be compared to the preciousness of time. What can diamonds do for us? Time, on the other hand, allows us to expand our wisdom-life, which is not only important to our current life, but also affects our future lives.

If we cherish time and contribute to society, then we are truly living. On the other hand, if we fail to use time properly, and instead merely pursue a living and fight for our own benefits, then we are no different than an animal or insect. To live a human life, we must be sensible, understanding, and know how to contribute to society. Only then will we be living a life worthy of a human.

Each of us should have aspirations and diligently work towards them. In this way, we can live a meaningful life. But achieving our goals requires time and hard work. Often we hear successful people say, "If only there were forty-eight hours in a day!" Clearly, success does require time and hard work.

Although we do develop plans to fulfill our dreams, we often let time pass us by due to a feeling in a single moment. Imagine that on a cold winter day we feel warm and cozy in bed. It is a struggle to get up. In this instant, we are the ones wasting our own precious time. No one hinders us, but we keep ourselves in delusion. Therefore, we are our own worst enemies. It is important for us to pull ourselves out of delusion. If we linger in the eddy of laziness, we simply fritter away our time.

I read a news report about a group of students who initiated a study retreat during the New Year's holiday. They asked a teacher to supervise and guide their schoolwork.

Five days later, when their study came to an end, a reporter asked them, "Everyone else relaxed and had fun over the holiday, yet you focused on your studies. How do you feel about that?"

One student replied, "Messing around during our vacation is a waste of time. We used our time to enrich our knowledge, so we actually gained five days." This kind of child truly knows how to cherish time.

There were also some parents who took their children sightseeing. The reporter asked one of the children, "Tomorrow you'll be back in school. Are you happy?"

The child answered, "No. I still have many places to visit. I wish the winter break were two months long. I don't like going back to school."

Both are students. Some prefer to enrich themselves, and others would rather play around and waste time.

Our lives demand that we develop a concept of managing time. Rather than idling time away, we should apply every moment to our family and to society. Take this elderly lady who lives in Taipei for instance. Her children are filial and pious, and wanted her to travel overseas as their gift to her on her sixtieth birthday. She said to them, "I am pleased that you are filial. But I prefer not to travel. Just give the money to me. I will donate it to Master Cheng Yen."

Her son continued to urge her. "Go on the trip! Everyone likes traveling abroad. You can always do good deeds later."

The elderly lady replied wisely, "You are encouraging me to travel abroad to make me happy, and your good intentions indeed have made me happy. But I will be even happier if I can help Tzu Chi do good deeds."

She donated the money to Tzu Chi and said to me, "Master, I am so grateful to walk the Tzu Chi path and have the opportunity to cultivate fields of blessings. I am also pleased that my filial children want me to travel overseas. Nonetheless, I still find that helping you build a hospital truly makes me happy."

The elderly lady truly understood how to use time and money, and wisely inferred what would allow her to achieve true happiness. If she had taken the trip, her happiness would have only lasted ten days and she would have been exhausted after the arduous travel. On the other hand, after the hospital is built it will save many lives and the hospital itself will last many decades or even a century. By taking the ten days saved for the trip and using the time to do charity work, she found true enjoyment through contributing and interacting with others.

We need to apply ourselves in the moments we are most needed. Some have asked me, "What is the value of life? How do we measure it?" I reply, "We cannot measure the value of life. It cannot be compared to that of money. In fact, life is priceless. The important thing is to use life appropriately so that it has value."

We are happy to talk about birth, yet we are somehow terrified to talk about death. Even some fragile elders on the verge of dying are still frightened and cannot accept the reality of death. Therefore, penetrating the truth of life has nothing to do with one's age. It is not important how long or how short we live. Confucius said, "If I learn the truth of life at dawn, I can die with no regrets at dusk!" If we hear words of truth and apply them in our lives, then we can die without regret.

With this in mind, there is no need for us to be concerned about the length of our life. The key is for us to understand the right way to deal with people and matters, and then apply it in our lives.

● **Labor and Leisure**

Nowadays we have more and more vacation time. This leads to many problems. For instance, many people may become bored by too much leisure time. They indulge in a lavish lifestyle and drink excessively. Consequently, they may cause accidents by driving drunk, get into trouble, or disturb the community for no reason.

There is a saying: "Idle men have no joy; busy men have no trouble." When we are busy, we have no time to cause trouble or become involved in disputes. Ordinary people often pursue a leisurely life. But would we be happy merely eating and doing nothing all day long? We travel around to sightsee, but will those beautiful scenes stay in our minds forever? No matter how majestic the landscape is, we cannot take it home. After the trip, we still face the same afflictions as before. What sort of happiness is this? Instead, if we genuinely dedicate ourselves to seizing each moment and helping the needy, then we will have indeed become living Bodhisattvas. As living Bodhisattvas, our minds and hearts will always be joyful and at ease at all times.

One day, when I was watching Da Ai News, I saw a reporter interviewing an old woman at a recycling center. This old woman had had a rough life. Even at her old age, she still had many challenges to overcome every day. The reporter asked her, "Don't you feel distressed by the many hardships you face?"

The old woman replied, "If I want to worry, I'll worry about meaningful things that can be resolved. Why should I worry about things that are meaningless and can't be resolved?" She is truly wise.

Most current social problems come from our inability to achieve inner harmony. So how do we keep our minds and hearts at peace? If we keep ourselves busy by doing more good deeds, then we will have no time for afflictions and disputes.

If we can take the care we give to our own family and extend that to all of society, then our minds and our views will be broadened. Witnessing the difficulties of others, we should reflect on our own lives and feel content. Thus, we will find balance for our minds, bodies, and emotions.

Those who are always doing good deeds can use their love and compassion to keep their emotions in balance. When they face impermanence, they can remind themselves to use their own willpower and courage to control their emotions so as not to commit foolish and regrettable acts. In other words, seizing every moment to do good deeds is like building an immune system for the mind, so that our minds will not be adversely influenced by a struggling economy, nor be infected by mental afflictions. If we take hold of time to discipline and cultivate our minds and bodies, our lives will be happy and blessed.

Mrs. Li has a strong, rigid personality. Her husband was in the military, so he was away from home most of the time. When she was younger, she had to raise the children all by herself. She handled all household matters alone, so she became very tough. Then, many years ago, she suffered a stroke and was partially paralyzed. This strong and independent person suddenly could not move about freely. How could she cope with this cruel reality? She developed a short temper and easily lost control of her emotions. Her relatives, friends, and neighbors stayed away from her.

When her father passed away, Tzu Chi volunteers chanted the Buddha's name at his funeral service. The volunteers approached her, got to know her, and brought her to visit the Jing Si Abode in Hualien. By taking my advice and watching Da Ai TV, she decided to become a Tzu Chi volunteer. She told everyone that watching Da Ai TV was rehabilitation for her mind and that doing volunteer work was physical therapy. She realized that, as a Tzu Chi volunteer, she could no longer lose her temper or yell at others.

Although she could not move around easily, she still walked with her cane through streets and alleys to collect recyclables, and paid no attention to the peculiar looks she got from others. She even went to the market to ask store owners for their used cartons. Witnessing her dedication to recycling and her change in temper, her neighbors were deeply touched: several joined her in recycling, and her husband also accompanied her to do volunteer work. This story shows that instead of asking others to change we should first change ourselves and rehabilitate our minds. Then our surrounding environment will change as well.

Once, an old lady suddenly felt dizzy while taking her morning walk. A Tzu Chi volunteer happened to pass by, and immediately rendered assistance. The volunteer hailed a cab to send her home and paid the cab fare for her. The old lady asked for the volunteer's name. He told her to just remember "Tzu Chi recycling center."

We often say that a *drop of kindness should be repaid with a flood of goodwill*. This old lady wanted to return the favor, so she located the recycling center and tried to find the volunteer to return the cab fare and thank him. She discovered, however, that everyone at the recycling center was a Tzu Chi volunteer. The volunteer who helped her did not want to claim credit for his good deed, so he did not identify himself. In order to pay back the kindness, the old lady became a volunteer at that recycling center. Originally she worked two or three hours a day. But the more she worked, the healthier she became, so she put in more and more hours. Eventually she worked from morning until evening and went home only at dusk.

Because of her illness, the old woman's filial children were worried. They could not bear to see her sort through piles of garbage for reusable materials. They disapproved of her doing recycling work. She asserted, however, that she did not want to be a patient; she would rather be a useful person and spend her days working. She emerged from her sickly life and brought out her inherent potential and ability. She was so busy working that she forgot about her illness and afflictions and was able to live a healthy and happy life. This shows that the more leisure time one has, the more the complaints and distractions.

I often see Tzu Chi volunteers give of themselves without any complaint or regret. Even when exhausted after a long day's work, they still insist that they are happy and grateful. Donating their labor and paying for their own expenses, they remain grateful and happy in their volunteering. This is "joyful giving." If you ask why they volunteer, they reply, "We are happy and willing." To give without asking for any return, or *to work willingly and accept the results joyfully,* is indeed admirable.

Section 2 – Crossing the Barrier of Each Second

It is an important Chinese tradition to celebrate the Lunar New Year. Most refer to this time as "crossing the barrier into another year." I feel like I am "crossing the barrier into another second" every day. Thoughts arise in our minds at every second and each thought may influence the rest of our life, so we should take hold of the present moment and pay attention to every second in order to take good care of our minds and move forward down the right path.

Sometimes our thoughts may deviate slightly and point us off the right path. Even the slightest deviation can lead us far astray. But when our thoughts are unwavering, our direction holds true.

● The Barriers of Years and Seconds

In the past, people became worried before Lunar New Year. For example, employees worried about being laid off, and debtors worried about being forced by their creditors to pay off debts. Since meeting a challenge is like "crossing a barrier," people had to "cross the barrier" into each year.

If we feel that crossing into another year every twelve months is full of anxiety and distress, is it not worse to have to cross the barrier into each second? What do I mean by this? We have a tendency to neglect the present moment until we make a mistake. Then we feel remorse about the wrongdoing we committed in that moment, or about hurting somebody or saying something inappropriate a month before, or even years before. If we had not been careless at those moments, we would not have felt sorrow and regret later.

At the moment we made the mistake, we failed to take care of our minds, so we feel regret afterwards. For instance, we feel remorse after failing a test. Why were we so nervous that we left so many questions unanswered? Why did we not study harder so that our minds would not have gone blank upon picking up the test? Because we do not train our minds to be calm every second, we lose control and become nervous when challenges arise.

We are disappointed in ourselves if we did not accomplish enough in the past. But what has passed is gone. If we continue to dwell on the past, angry at ourselves for not training enough, for saying or doing the wrong things, we will lose the present by constantly looking back.

On the other hand, if we forget about the past and concentrate only on the future, we ignore the present. I have said, "The past is a distraction; the future is an illusion." The important thing is to pay attention to this moment, to the here and now. A certain cause produces a certain effect. If we create errant causes, then we reap bad results. Therefore, to cross the barrier into each second, we must seize the present moment to complete the work at hand, and disregard what the future may bring. We should not speak ill words, commit wrongdoings, or miss opportunities.

"Crossing a barrier" is a positive attitude with which to meet a challenge. We should maintain a positive outlook, otherwise we can easily become lazy and degenerate. "Crossing the barrier into each new second" is to alert ourselves that we must treasure time. We should race with time to ensure that we do not waste our lives. We must be mindful at all times, and brave the challenges of human relations.

There is a Ms. Huang who was still a child when she emigrated with her parents to Sweden. When she grew up, she got married, and worked hard with her husband in the restaurant business. She learned about Tzu Chi while watching Da Ai TV. A few years ago she came back to Taiwan for a visit and came to the Jing Si Abode in Hualien. She was deeply impressed and vowed to become a Tzu Chi volunteer.

Not long after Ms. Huang returned to Sweden, two Taiwanese tourists had a swimming accident there. One drowned and the other was rescued. Since these two tourists were alone and far from home, no one knew how to handle the situation, so Tzu Chi headquarters in Taiwan was contacted for assistance.

Tzu Chi volunteers hastily contacted Ms. Huang, asking her to help. She was very nervous when she was assigned the case. She had never helped strangers before and suddenly she was to handle such a major incident. Nevertheless, she immediately changed her perspective: since she had made a vow to become a Tzu Chi volunteer, she summoned up her courage to take the case. After some searching, she finally located the hospital where the survivor was being treated, and offered her comfort and company. She also helped take care of all the issues related to the accident until the survivor and the ashes of the deceased returned to Taiwan.

Every big tree starts from a tiny seed, so we should never take lightly even the smallest of intentions. I once read a news report about a tragedy. An Asian man moved to New York City. He was hired by a large company and lived a comfortable life there. But he was laid off some time later. His thoughts went astray for one moment. He took a gun to the immigration office and took hostages. When the police surrounded him, he shot and killed more than ten people. In the end, he also killed himself.

We should always look inward and reflect upon ourselves. If we always complain and bicker, that is because our thoughts have not crossed over the barriers, and we have planted bad karmic seeds. It is unlikely that everyone and everything we encounter in our lives are pleasant, or that every action and every word are to our liking. We should take every opportunity to train and test ourselves with whatever we encounter. When facing adversity, we should try to prevent any negative thoughts from arising, and even feel grateful toward our antagonists. If we do this, we can commend ourselves for having a clear mind and inner peace, and for not letting ourselves be hindered by adversity.

We should always reflect on ourselves instead of judging others. When we are displeased with other people's behavior, we must control ourselves and remember that their way of thinking and their actions are only an expression of this particular instant. With this kind of mentality, their words and behavior will not upset us, and we will be able to overcome the barrier of this second, and the barriers set forth by our hearts.

Moreover, our lives cannot be separated from external conditions. If we always possess a discriminating mind, we will create insurmountable barriers by not accepting certain conditions. For example, in the winter, a cup of hot tea makes us feel warm and comfortable. Yet in the heat of summer, we would immediately reject the same cup of hot tea. This is also a barrier of the second that we encounter in our daily lives. If we always pay attention to the barriers of each minute and each second, then we can safely overcome the barrier of ignorance.

As the Lunar New Year approaches, everyone wants the coming year to be a good one, but we must first live our days well. To live our days well, we must lead a virtuous life by doing good deeds often. This is because doing good deeds makes us happy every day, thus every day is a good day to us and every year is a good year.

● Eighty-six Thousand Four Hundred Seconds

Everybody says there are twenty-four hours in a day, yet I prefer to count my days as 86,400 seconds each. When I pass every second in earnest, I feel fulfilled. It is said, "Good or bad, this moment exists only for an instant." There is no need to differentiate this moment from that moment. Once a moment has passed, it will never return, nor can we foresee what will happen in the future. It is most important for us to seize this very second, because only this instant is real.

A wasted day is worth less than a meaningful second. There are 86,400 seconds in a day. If we do nothing during the whole day, that day is wasted. However, if we can make the best use of one second, we can at least make good use of 1/86,400 of that day and gain something from it.

We must safeguard every minute and every second of our life. Can we accept 86,399 seconds as a full day? Of course not. Every few years, a leap second is added to or subtracted from the Coordinated Universal Time (UTC) to keep its time of day close to the mean solar time. This shows that we cannot miscalculate even one second. We must make each second count. If we live by the second, we will certainly cherish each and every moment. If we live by the day, then we will think that after today we still have tomorrow, and after this year we still have next year. If we are not careful, time can easily be wasted.

Indulging in pleasure and comfort is not only wasteful, it may create bad karma from erroneous thoughts. As we know, bad karma will negatively influence our next life as well. On the other hand, if we use time appropriately, we create positive karma: good, healthy seeds. Ultimately we will accumulate virtues and merits for ourselves.

It is with great fortune that we were born as humans in this life. We must understand that *time is as precious as gold, yet gold cannot buy time.* There was once a boy living in the mountains of Alishan who was innocent and studious. Each day he walked for more than an hour to attend school. His family was poor, but he was forgiving and understanding, and he knew how to make good use of his time.

Every day after school, the very first thing he did was to help his grandmother with household chores. His mother had come to Taiwan from a foreign country to marry his father, but she left after giving birth to him. Still, he never complained. When people asked why his mother abandoned him, he would reply with a smile, "Mother had her reasons." He was grateful to his grandmother for taking care of him. Seeing how his grandmother's back gradually hunched lower year after year, he realized that he had to take hold of time to be filial to his grandmother.

His grandmother grew and sold vegetables for a living, so he had learned to cook when he was a third grader in primary school. After school he would rush home to prepare dinner because he wanted to have a hot meal ready for his grandmother when she arrived. What a mature and considerate child!

The boy's uncle had mental problems. If he came home and saw the boy doing homework under a lamp, he would turn the lamp off and scold the boy for wasting electricity. The boy was aware of his uncle's problems, so he never complained. Instead, he tried to finish his chores as early as possible, so he could do his homework before it got dark. Sometimes he had to do his homework under a street lamp. Although he encountered tremendous difficulties, he never missed an assignment.

When he was asked, "What do you wish you could tell your mother?" he replied, "I wish I could tell Mother to come home soon, so Grandmother wouldn't worry about her."

When asked, "What worries you the most?" he replied, "That Grandmother can't sell all of her vegetables, because if she cannot sell all the vegetables she gets very worried."

"What is your wish?"

"I wish Father would come home, so I could cook for him."

This child was truly very considerate and adorable.

There is a poem that says, "Yesterday is gone; I cannot keep it. Today is full of worries; my mind is troubled." The past has gone, and we cannot keep even a second. Today is full of things that bother us. What a regrettable life this is. Why do we not simply seize this moment to learn more good things and do more good deeds?

● **Cross the Threshold with Equanimity**

Living in this world, we are constantly in contact with people and involved in affairs. We cannot always have what we want, nor can everything go as planned. This is the reality of life. Despite this, we should do our best when we are physically capable. We must also take good care of our minds. In doing so, we will not be disturbed or distracted by worldly matters, and we will be able to deal with our ever-changing surroundings.

The ability to endure hardship enables us to overcome all adversities. With a joyful and respectful attitude toward others, we can accept their undesirable behaviors, or even influence them to change by setting a good example ourselves. In this way, we can cross the barrier of every second. Conversely, if we lack equanimity and regard things with discrimination, we will feel pain and be in constant unrest.

There was once a man learning swordplay in Japan who implored a famous master to teach him. He asked the master, "If I want to be a successful swordsman, what type of mindset should I maintain? How should I handle myself when an opponent thrusts his sword at me?"

The master replied, "If you maintain the attitude of 'crossing the threshold', you can master the art of swordplay and handle yourself well when facing your opponent's sword."

Most Japanese buildings have sliding doors, so a carpenter installs a trough for the two sections of door to slide in. How hard can it be to cross over this threshold? Why is it that merely by maintaining the mindset of crossing a threshold, one can defeat his opponent? We all know that it is quite dangerous to practice swordplay when real swords are used. With a moment's distraction or a small mistake, the swordsman will be injured. It is a matter of life and death.

When dealing with life and death situations, we sometimes become so nervous that we fail. The mindset of crossing the threshold is equanimity. If we constantly maintain a mind of equanimity, we can handle any crisis. Occasionally we will run into difficult situations in our daily lives, but as long as we maintain a mind of equanimity, then at every moment, we will be able to cross the barrier of each second with ease. In other words, cultivating spirituality is indeed part of daily life.

In August 2009, Typhoon Morakot caused severe damage in Taiwan. The grief felt by survivors was beyond words. I am grateful that Tzu Chi volunteers immediately mobilized to bring care and warmth to the survivors. Some of the volunteers were victims themselves, yet they maintained their composure in the face of danger and helped others in need. Ms. Guo is a Tzu Chi volunteer who lives in the Liugui Mountain area. Before the typhoon hit, she came down from the mountain to help out in the Tzu Chi typhoon emergency center. The unexpected windstorm damaged roads and disrupted traffic, and since her husband and parents-in-law were still on the mountain, she was very anxious. Nonetheless, she tried her best to compose herself.

At the center, many people were worried sick about their families in the mountains. The situation was chaotic. Ms. Guo stepped forward to console and soothe everyone there. She said, "My family is in the mountains too. At this moment, we should remain calm and pray sincerely." Her spirit was truly extraordinary. Later, her mother-in-law was rescued and transported down from the mountain by helicopter. When she saw Ms. Guo, she kept saying, "I was terrified." Ms. Guo hugged her and patted her back, saying, "It's OK, you're safe."

The next day Ms. Guo saw her mother-in-law leaving the local Tzu Chi Office, so she asked where she was going.

"I am going to the shelter," replied the mother-in-law.

"Didn't you just come down from the mountains yesterday?"

She said, "I am going to help comfort everyone there."

This elder was able to let go of her worries and gather her strength to console others. When she saw survivors coming out of the helicopter or people anxiously waiting for their families, she would go hug them, saying, "In situations like this, we must be strong. I just came down from the mountains yesterday. People in the mountains are all safe."

When encountering obstacles, we must not lose our calm, for we all possess innate potential and wisdom. Mr. Chen is a Tzu Chi volunteer in Nantou County. He watched helplessly as the flood washed away his farmland, yet he still rushed to join others in the disaster relief efforts.

Someone asked him, "Your tomato patch was washed away by the flood. What will you do?"

He said, "Right now it is more important to rescue people. We shouldn't think about anything else." *He truly lived by the saying, When we take one step forward, we must lift the other foot from the ground so as to move onward.*

Mr. Chen learned and practiced Tzu Chi's teachings in his daily life. As a Tzu Chi volunteer, he understood what time and which talent to use in a certain situation, and the mentality required to reconcile his dilemmas. His story is truly touching.

Section 3 – A Moment Becomes a Lifetime

When I took refuge in my early twenties, my master, the Venerable Dharma Master Yin Shun was still in his fifties. It feels like it just happened not long ago. Time has passed nonstop since then, but one thing I still remember vividly: when I knelt down to take refuge, Master Yin Shun told me, "Our affinity as master and disciple is very rare and special. I cannot say much to you since it is almost time for the ordination, but you must always remember to work for Buddhism and for all living beings."

"For Buddhism and for all living beings": those words took less than one second to say, yet I was deeply moved. I took the passage to heart, turning that moment into eternity. Those words have stayed with me all my life. We must apply Buddhist teachings in our daily lives. If we can follow the Dharma at every second in everything we do, we will *seize the present moment and make it everlasting* as we create blessing and virtue in every moment.

● The Moment We Make a Vow

In every second of every day, we must seize the opportunity to give and form good affinities with others. There is a story that took place in Europe, where winter is very cold with frequent snow. One day it snowed heavily. A young man was watching television and listening to music, when his father came over and patted his shoulder. He said "My son, do you like that music?"

"Yes, I do."

The father asked, "After listening to that music, how long can you remember it?"

The young man was surprised and did not know how to answer. His father then asked, "Would you like to do something unforgettable, something that will make you happy each time you remember it?"

He asked, "What is this thing that's so special?"

The father pointed to the house next door and said, "Last night it snowed heavily again. The elderly lady living alone next door has not been out to the grocery store for days. Could you go help her shovel the sidewalk in front of her house?"

The young man thought it over and said, "Alright. It's no big deal to shovel snow." So he took a shovel and went next door.

After shoveling the snow, he came back home. Soon he saw the elderly lady open the door and stick her head out. When she saw that her walkway was clear, she smiled happily. She took a basket and carefully walked out of her house. The father stood next to the young man and asked, "Do you see that? The old lady is able to leave her house now."

The young man turned and hugged his father happily. He said, "Thank you, Dad. You made me realize that helping others is a joy."

Twenty years later, this young man had his own children. So he told his son the story. He had never forgotten his father's teaching. The elderly neighbor's expression at seeing the walkway in front of her house cleared of snow was a constant reminder for him: when someone smiles contentedly from the heart, that is the most beautiful face there is.

Spiritual cultivation and good deeds can actually be done in our daily lives. When we maintain a kind heart and make good use of time to do what we are supposed to do, our minds will be at ease and our lives will be beautiful and fulfilling. However, it is easy to be enthusiastic but difficult to be persistent. Sometimes we are touched when we see people help others, and when we hear of good deeds we want to participate as well. But these are often passions of the moment. It is difficult to achieve anything with just short-lived enthusiasm. Therefore, *we must seize that moment and make it everlasting.*

What does it mean to *"seize that moment and make it everlasting?"* A moment is the short time when a thought arises. It does not take long to make a vow. Once a good thought arises, we must bear in mind the thought and the commitment we made and make them everlasting, life after life. If we can always hold on to each moment's good thought, we will benefit from it our entire life.

To accomplish a good deed, all the conditions must be ripe. The most important thing is to seize the moment, grab the opportunity, and do it in a timely manner. We should always maintain our aspirations, then we can make best use of our lives. I once lived in Tzuyun Temple for a period of time. Back then I did a lot of farm work, such as planting, weeding, and harvesting rice. I remember once, when I was weeding, I stood on the ridge of the rice paddy and looked over the entire field. The paddy was only about two-and-a-half acres, but it appeared endless. It was early spring, and the water in the paddy was freezing. I could not help but feel it was impossible to finish weeding this huge rice paddy.

But I changed my thinking right away, telling myself that if something is right, we should just do it. So I started to weed the area my hands could reach, and focused on the work in front of me. I did not waste any time thinking about how big the paddy was. I concentrated on the area right in front of me and worked diligently one step at a time. Finally, I finished weeding the entire rice paddy.

On the path of life, if we can help others in a timely manner, our wisdom-life will grow. On the other hand, if we do nothing and merely idle away our time, our wisdom-life will stop growing. Therefore, *the more we do, the more we gain, and both our wisdom and blessings will grow. The less we do, the more we lose, and both our wisdom and blessings will wither.* Let us take hold of our good thoughts and do the best we can.

From ancient times to the present day, is history not an accumulation of moments? In life, we must always be mindful of making the best use of time and always apply that mindfulness in everything we do. When we act, we gain. When we do, we feel. Life's history is written by seizing this moment now.

● **A Lifetime Goal**

On the fortieth anniversary of the founding of Tzu Chi, a Tzu Chi volunteer came to see me and said, "A Buddhist master asked me to bring you this message."

"What is it?"

He said, "It is not easy to live for forty years. To have passed forty years safely is really no small feat."

After thinking carefully, I felt that these words had profound meaning. It is hard to choose the right path in life. Even when we are on the right path, it is not easy to have followers. Forty-some years since the founding of Tzu Chi is no short time. Looking back to the starting point, I see that Tzu Chi has not strayed even slightly from its original course. This makes me feel that everything has been worthwhile.

How many decades are there in our lifespan? Once we aim in the right direction, we must diligently charge forward. Many things will naturally accumulate. Several years ago, a strong earthquake shook Iran and caused many casualties. Tzu Chi volunteers rushed to disaster areas to help the survivors. The volunteers provided free clinics while they assessed the earthquake damage, but due to the language barrier and the unfamiliar locale, they encountered great difficulty in their disaster relief efforts in the beginning. An Iranian military doctor saw the blue and white uniforms that volunteers wore and thought he had seen them before.

He asked, "Do you have a television channel?"

The volunteers answered that they had Da Ai TV.

"That's right, It must be that channel. I often see your volunteers wearing this uniform and doing good deeds in many places." Some of Da Ai's programs provided English subtitles, so he understood them. He continued, "There is a teacher who often speaks on that channel, and she really makes a lot of sense."

It is their custom to show respect to someone by calling that person "teacher." Mr. Chen, a Tzu Chi volunteer in Jordan, showed that military doctor my picture on his prayer beads and asked, "Is this person the teacher you are talking about?"

"Yes, it is."

As he learned about Tzu Chi from interacting with the volunteers, whenever volunteers wanted to introduce Tzu Chi to locals or take care of some business, this doctor served as their interpreter. Because of his help, these volunteers were able to go about their work in Iran unhindered.

For Tzu Chi to be recognized around the world as an organization that does good work, I am grateful not only to Da Ai TV for publicizing it, but also to the volunteers all over the world who help the needy and relieve the suffering in their blue and white uniforms. Without needing much explanation, everyone can see the results of their hard work: achievements which have accumulated over time.

Accumulating good seeds over a lifetime enables our wisdom-life to grow and creates blessings for our next lives. There is a well-known Buddhist story about a very determined monk named Tetsugen Doko who lived hundreds of years ago in Japan. He dedicated himself to spreading Buddhist teachings, and vowed to raise funds to carve sutras on wooden slabs, so that Buddhist teachings could be widely circulated.

One winter, a big blizzard struck Japan and the entire capital was covered with snow and ice. In order to raise funds, Tetsugen Doko often stood on the Kamo River Bridge of the major road to the capital, asking passersby to make a donation. Although the weather was freezing cold and the biting wind made him shiver, he still spoke loudly to solicit donations.

Some passersby who saw the monk working so hard admired his dedication and made donations. Others looked at him in cold detachment or simply ignored him. One day a samurai rode by on a horse. The monk said to the samurai, "I am Tetsugen Doko. I made a vow to carve the Tripitaka. These sutras are important to us because they can purify people's minds and save the human race. Please make a donation."

The samurai could not believe that an individual could raise enough money, one or two pennies at a time, to finish such a big project of carving the Tripitaka. He thought it impossible, so he rode off. But Tetsugen Doko did not give up. He ran after the samurai, saying, "Please make a pledge and help me fulfill this worthy vow. Even if you only donate a penny, I will still be very grateful." To stop the monk's pestering, the samurai threw a penny into his alms bowl. When he saw the snow-covered monk bow respectfully to thank him, he was deeply touched.

Later, all the snow melted, causing serious floods. Many homes were damaged. People lost their livelihoods. Hungry and cold, their lives hung in the balance. Tetsugen Doko could not bear to see their suffering, so he used the funds he had saved for inscribing the sutras to buy rice to help the victims. Eventually he used up all the funds he had collected.

After the disaster, Tetsugen Doko went out again to raise funds for inscribing the sutras. Some admired his kind heart and made donations, but others were not as understanding. They thought he was swindling them in the name of inscribing sutras. Although Tetsugen Doko was slandered, insulted, scolded, and even had rocks thrown at him, he still firmly upheld his vows and kept collecting donations.

Tetsugen Doko planned to hire one hundred skilled engravers to carve on sixty thousand slabs of cherry wood for this huge project. The samurai overheard this news and was shocked. He thought to himself, "This monk is truly great. In order to help the disaster victims, he stopped the sutra project. He had to endure insults and raise funds from the public all over again." The samurai made a vow to help the monk fulfill his dream as soon as possible.

The samurai had sixty thousand slabs of cherry wood shipped to Tetsugen Doko from Nara. With this gift, the sutra project was finally on track. It took seventeen years to complete the carving of all the sutras, which was the first complete copy of the Tripitaka in Japan. It is said that the sixty thousand slabs of cherry wood on which the scriptures were engraved have been preserved to this day. Many classic sutras have been printed from these slabs. This great project was accomplished because of Tetsugen Doko's tremendous willpower and determination.

Where there is compassion, there is virtue; where there is a will, there is a way. It is important to have perseverance and willpower. Once we are inspired to make a vow and set our life in the right direction, we must hold on to our original vows and carry them out throughout our lifetime.

Chapter 3 - Making Each Moment Count

People often say there is not enough time. Time is truly empty and formless. We cannot touch it or grab it. Whether we can get the most out of time depends on how we use and allocate it.

A Malaysian student once gave me a glass jar as a gift. The jar was filled with rocks and pebbles. He told me the story of the jar.

One day his teacher had taken him and some other students on a field trip. The teacher picked up some rocks from the ground and put them into a jar one by one. When the jar was nearly full, the teacher asked the students if there was still enough room for more.

"Yes," a student replied, as he picked up some small pebbles to put in. The jar indeed held more.

The teacher asked, "Is there any more room?"

Another student said, "Yes, there is." He put in some fine-grained sand. The jar was soon filled.

"Can it hold more?" the teacher asked.

"No, there is no more space," the students replied.

"Don't forget, it can still hold water," the teacher told them.

The student told us what he had learned from this field trip: we should prioritize everything. The rocks in the jar are like main tasks, and the small pebbles secondary tasks. We should do the main tasks first, then the secondary tasks; after that, we should allocate our time wisely, and not forget what we are supposed to do.

Modern life is hurried and busy. If we do not understand the concept of time, or how to manage and use it, then time will use us. We must take control of our time; then we can progress equally in both our career and our mission in life.

 Section One – Calculating the Time of Life

Consumers make up most of today's society, so I will calculate the time of life from this perspective. Generally speaking, we are already consumers and beneficiaries before the age of twenty. Only after twenty do we start to contribute to society and to others. After sixty, we retire from the work force and again depend on social resources and the protection of our families. Some people even waste their whole lives on eating, drinking, and playing.

Sometimes I hear volunteers say, "I'm very busy," but I tell them, "Being busy is a blessing; if you have nothing to do, then you're in trouble." Either having nothing to do or doing nothing is troublesome because the value of life lies in what we do. When you really think about it, we do not have much time in which to help others.

● Use Only One-third of our Lives

One day a Tzu Chi volunteer brought her son to see me. "What is your major?" I asked him. He told me it was economics.

"Then you must be good at arithmetic," I said. "Can you calculate how much time there is in life?"

The boy did not seem to understand my question, so I asked in a different way, "How many hours do you sleep every day?"

"Eight hours," he replied.

"How many hours do you study?"

"About eight hours also."

"What do you do for the remaining eight hours?" He smiled, but did not reply.

"Sleeping eight hours seems long," I told him. "It is a shame if your remaining eight hours are spent resting and doing nothing. It shows that you don't know how to calculate life's economic value. The world economy rises and falls; sometimes we lose and sometimes we win. However, if time slips away, it is lost forever. That is why I am always considering how to economize the time in my life."

Let us measure the time in our lives. If we sleep eight hours per day, that means one-third of the day is spent sleeping. If a person lives to sixty, then twenty years will have been spent sleeping and not interacting with the outside world. In addition, there are our innocent childhood and school years, roughly twenty years also. Furthermore, if we need forty minutes to eat a meal, then we spend two hours on three meals per day. That is more than seven hundred hours spent on eating in a year. These are actual hours we need to spend, and we have not yet included relaxing, playing, and idling. How much time is left to devote to the benefit of mankind?

We should learn life economy, and not be so hung up on the economy of assets. There is a common saying, "Man proposes; God disposes." It is a hard life if we painstakingly calculate every penny. Some people toil all their lives to improve their financial situation at the price of their own health. In the end, what did they achieve? Business is not without karmic consequence; the bigger the business, the larger the karmic debt.

We should be content with having enough food and clothing, and not be vain and greedy. The important thing is to fully use our abilities for the good of others. In the old days, most people were not wealthy or well-educated. Elder siblings had to help their parents look after the younger siblings, and even work as child laborers to supplement their family income. But people in those days were willing to work hard at a young age to help their family and contribute to society.

Let us take a look at today's situation. Devoted parents do their best to raise and educate their children, and social resources are abundant at our disposal. Yet how much time does each person spend giving back to the community?

● The Four-year-old Elder

All historical events are stored in the treasure chest of time. For those who do not utilize time wisely, however, time may become an abyss of evil.

There is a seventy-eight-year-old man who sweeps the streets every morning. In the still dawn, the crisp sound of his broom scraping over the ground is like a beautiful melody, and the clean streets he leaves behind bring joy to all who pass by.

One day the old man was sweeping when someone asked how old he was. He held out four fingers. The man asked again, "Are you seventy-four or eighty-four years old?"

"Neither," he answered, "I am only four years old."

His neighbors were puzzled. Why did he say he was only four years old? The old man explained, "I have lived for seventy-eight years, but if you only count the time I have been really useful, I am only four years old."

He told everyone, "The first seventy years of my life was like a dream; I lived in vain. After age seventy, I finally woke up from my delusional slumber. Of the eight years after that, once you eliminate the time spent on eating, sleeping, and relaxing, only four years were really spent working and can count toward a meaningful life. Based on that calculation, I am only four years old. I am fortunate to have woken up in time to understand that time is the treasury where merits and virtues are accumulated. I have already wasted seventy years; I must hurry and accomplish what I can. It appears that I am sweeping the streets, but I am actually cleansing my own mind."

This old man only learned to live after realizing the true meaning of life. Not only did he dismiss the years he lived in delusion, he also subtracted the time spent on sleeping and eating. He only counted the time spent benefiting himself and others as his true age. The true value of life lies in utilizing the physical body to help and benefit others. If we only enjoy ourselves and use Earth's resources without contributing anything to society or the human race, then we are merely consumers. From the Buddhist point of view, we are cancelling our own blessings.

The Buddha came to this world to teach and to relieve the suffering of all sentient beings, not to ease the lives of us humans. If we idle away our lives, we are no different from other sentient beings, such as chickens, ducks, worms, and ants. It is a rare opportunity to be born as humans in this world. We must bear witness to our era and leave something for history. Yesterday's work is today's history, and today's work will be tomorrow's history. If we do the right thing well, our footprints will become worthy enough to be recorded into history.

● Adding Twenty Years to Life

No one knows whether our life will be long or short. Actually, life is not about its length, it is about how you use it and how you enhance its value. Even if you live to a very old age, it is useless if you have not brought out life's true value. And who can live forever? The Buddha Himself only lived eighty years, of which forty-nine years were used to the fullest extent. These were the most useful years of his life.

I remember many years ago a woman told me her husband had passed away. She was so devastated that she wanted to die with him. I asked her what did her husband do and how old he was when he passed.

"He was a doctor; he was sixty years old when he died," she replied. "My husband was a very good doctor. Other people work eight hours a day, but my husband worked almost sixteen hours. He would open his clinic early in the morning and work until eleven or twelve at night. Sometimes he did not have time to eat. If patients knocked on our door at midnight for treatment, he would take care of them just the same."

"He worked sixteen hours a day to take care of his patients," I said, "All this to save lives. He was indeed a good doctor."

"They say good people live long; why did he die at sixty?" The woman sobbed as she asked.

I said to her, "Your husband's lifespan was longer than sixty years, because life's value is determined by how one uses his life. Others work eight hours a day, but your husband spent sixteen hours to benefit humankind. Therefore the value of his life is twice that of others. Based on this calculation, his life was worth at least eighty years. You should be happy for him and bless him since he lived his life to the fullest; he had no regrets."

After hearing my words, the woman stopped weeping and smiled, as her eyes lit up. "My husband did make good use of his time; his life was truly worthwhile."

Living in this world, we must rid ourselves of desires and selfishness. Only when we live for others will we be at peace and achieve life's fullest value. This is truly living.

Ordinary people yearn for longevity, yet is it a blessing to live a long life? There is a 137-year-old man in India, possibly the oldest living person in the world. He is very healthy, but he often says, "God has forgotten about me!" He is sad because all his friends have passed away one by one. Even his own children and grandchildren, and many of his friends' children and grandchildren, died before him. He said that many people have forgotten about him; the world seems to forget his existence. He must be very lonely.

The true measure of life lies not in its longevity. Rather than searching for ways to live longer, why do we not pragmatically bring out the value of life and live life to its fullest? In doing so, we will experience true longevity. Once we begin to live a meaningful life, we expand our life's value twofold or even tenfold. As a result, a sixty-year-old person's life can be worth six hundred years. When we steadfastly make prudent use of every moment in our life, we can say our life is endless.

Section Two – Racing Against Time

Sometimes when guests eat meals with me at Jing Si Abode, they ask me why I eat so fast. I reply that I do not have enough time. I hear some people spend three hours to eat a meal, yet I strive to save time while eating.

I read an article about Zen Master Baizhang. When it was his turn to perform the duty of burning incense, he had to wake up early and strike a wooden board to wake up others, then tidy up the main hall. One morning, he woke up and realized that he overslept by five minutes. He was extremely sorry for his negligence. He rushed to strike the board and tidy the main hall, but the morning worship was subsequently delayed five minutes. After morning worship, the Zen master prostrated himself and repented in front of the five hundred monks in the monastery. He said, "There are five hundred people in the monastery. I wasted five minutes of each person's time. How much time have I wasted for all five hundred people?"

I was deeply impressed by this article. Decades later, I still remember this story clearly. That is why I often race against time and conscientiously seize every moment. I do not let a single moment slip by, and I do things pragmatically step by step.

● **Keep a Good Routine**

Today people are so busy that they work and rest at odd hours and sometimes reverse day and night, falling into an irregular schedule. When we work, we should work hard every moment and rest when it is time to rest in order to save energy for the next day's work. The time in our life is precious. We should not waste valuable daylight hours dawdling around. We should separate day and night, separate working hours from resting hours, and keep a regular daily routine.

Living in this world, our schedule should follow nature's course. When the sun rises, we should wake up and get ready for the day's work, each person keeping his post. At sundown, we should wrap up our work and head home, which is the happiest hour for the family.

Time is short. We should learn how to manage our time. There is a woman in Kaohsiung whose husband did not take responsibility for the family after they got married. The woman became the sole breadwinner, taking care of the children and working hard to maintain a normal life. It must have been truly difficult to provide for her family and raise her children on her own.

Unfortunately, while in her thirties she was diagnosed with cancer. Shortly afterward, her doctor also found a tumor in her thyroid. She was tormented by these ailments. Faced with an uncaring husband and young children at home, she still continued to work and take care of her family. She bravely fought against time with her ailing body. More than ten years ago she joined

Tzu Chi and learned of Buddhist teachings. She realized that it was a blessing to still be able to work. Since then, she has never complained about her fate. If *we work willingly and accept the results joyfully,* our mind will be at ease.

Day after day, the woman saw rich people complaining about lacking fame and social status. She saw famous and powerful people discontent at not having smart and well-behaved children. There are so many complaints and demands. She always thought to herself: everyone lacks so much, I lack nothing except time.

When you feel that you do not have enough time, you are leading a positive life. On the other hand, if you feel you have all the time in the world, then your life is likely wasted on sluggishness and emptiness. Although a cancer patient, this Tzu Chi volunteer works two jobs to support her family. Each day she works at a co-op and a lunchbox factory. How much time does she still have? No one knows. Not only must she raise and educate her young children, she also needs time to fulfill her vow to walk the Bodhisattva path.

How does she manage her time? She leaves home at six o'clock each morning to collect recyclables. Hot or cold, rain or shine, she walks the streets picking up cardboard boxes, plastic bottles, and aluminum cans. She returns home to organize all that she has collected and then does chores around the house. Afterwards, she leaves home to work at her two hourly jobs. Upon finishing both jobs by three o'clock in the afternoon, she goes out again to collect more recyclables until dark. Such is her daily life.

Even though she is poor and lives a frugal life, she willingly accepts her destiny without regrets. She is using her time to its absolute fullest. Someone once said to her, "You work all day long like a spinning top. You don't even get enough sleep. You are abusing yourself."

She replied, "It's not like that at all. I sleep less to make more time available for myself. The Master has said, 'When you feel tired, switching to another task is a way of resting.'"

The woman works hard to make a living, and does recycling as a way to rest. She equates walking down the street with circumambulating the Buddha in spiritual meditation, and sees bending down to pick up recyclables as bowing down to the Buddha in respect. Whatever she does, she keeps the Buddha in her heart. What a full life she leads!

Some people have advised her to take advantage of modern medicine and consider surgery to cure her illness. She answers, "No need. I have already signed up to be a body donor when I die. Meanwhile, I will work however long I can."

This volunteer has had a rough life, yet she never complains. She knows how to use her time wisely. Her life is a classic example of taking the modern sutras to heart; I truly admire her.

Today, advanced technology has brought much convenience to humans, allowing us to save lots of time. However, there are people who have lost their sense of direction by misusing technology. This makes me wonder whether technology is making our lives easier or simply confusing us. It all depends on how you see it, and one's point of view can be adjusted.

A college student once shared his experience with us. He said, "In the past, I used to idle away my time doing nothing. During these past few days in the Jing Si Abode, I have woken up even earlier than I used to go to bed. But I feel my time is well spent and my day is full." We must take hold of time and work diligently. Once the work is done we can reap the results. On the other hand, if we reverse day and night and idle away our time, it is a great pity indeed.

● Immerse in the Dharma at Dawn

People often see death as eternal sleep. Actually, our nightly slumber is like temporary death. An eternal sleep lasts until the next life; a temporary death lasts until the next day. Many people are diligent and start their recycling work before dawn. I asked them why they start so early. They tell me, "Master, you have said that our lifetime is limited. The longer we sleep, the more time we waste; the more deeds we do, the more virtue we gain." It all depends on how you think.

Life is a precious opportunity, but if we spend our time resting and sleeping, we are wasting life. We accumulate virtue only by utilizing our time to give. Sleeping too much is no rest at all; the next day we feel heavy and ache all over. The more we sleep, the groggier we become. Consequently, we are unable to think clearly.

When we see someone looking dazed, we often ask him if he is fully awake, because although he may be awake, his brain is still sleeping and his mind is cloudy. Even though he is in contact with the outside world, he cannot hear others, nor can he distinguish truth from deception or good from evil.

Some people think that since they are neither greedy nor irritable, there is no harm in sleeping a bit longer. Exactly because they do not consider themselves to be wrong, they remain lost in delusion without knowing it. This does no good for their physical life or their wisdom-life. We all have a clear innate wisdom. It is a great pity if we cannot keep our heads in everyday life, and utilize that wisdom in all our encounters. We should not live just to consume. We should cherish our wisdom-life and dedicate ourselves to serving humanity.

Even if we take no action to advance ourselves and just stay put, time will still flow past us and our bodies will age and deteriorate. Therefore, we should make good use of our abilities while we are mentally and physically fit.

I once heard a doctor suggest that people should eat to eighty-percent full and no more. We can also apply this concept to sleep. Sleeping six hours should be enough. Let us strive to live life to the fullest. Use a quarter of the day to sleep, half to give and serve humanity, and the remaining quarter will be more than enough to eat and relax.

I once read a magazine article about "morning people," which promoted waking up early for its mental and physical benefits. While others say early to bed and early to rise, I say late to bed but early to rise. If we go to bed before eleven o'clock at night—since there are twenty-four hours in a day, eleven o'clock is the same as twenty-three o'clock—this is "going to bed late." Getting out of bed at five o'clock in the morning is "rising early." With this habit, one cannot sleep so much as to become dazed and lazy.

It may be difficult to get up early at first, but it can be done. First turn your body over, then think about something else. After getting up, you will feel happy and energetic. We should train ourselves to be self-conscious and alert. When it is time to wake up, we should wake up; when it is time to rest, we should rest. Always be alert and take notice of our thoughts and thought patterns, so that these habits can become an integral part of our daily life.

A couple once brought their son to see me. They told me their son did not sleep all night because he was surfing the internet. I asked the young man, "Why don't you sleep?"

"I do," he replied.

I told him, "You stay up too late. Can you go to bed earlier?"

He replied mischievously, "I do go to bed early: at five or six in the morning."

The rise of the Internet brought forth two entirely different phenomena: one is the lure leading people on a deluded path. Glued to the computer all night, they are exhausted during the day. They are either drowsy in class or dazed at work, and their lives are seriously affected. The other is the broadening of people's views toward the world, and their expansion of knowledge. Therefore, we must guide our children to the right path and benefit from correct use of technology.

A group of Tzu Chi college students uses the Internet to connect with youths in other countries and promote the Immerse in the Dharma at Dawn Movement. The participants turn on their computers at 5:30 AM and watch the live broadcast of "Wisdom at Dawn" on Da Ai Television together. The program shows the morning teaching that I have just delivered in the main hall of the Jing Si Abode. In addition to their studies at school, these young students watch the program attentively every morning and take notes. They diligently study the Buddhist teachings in hopes of increasing their wisdom.

After participating in Immerse in the Dharma at Dawn online, these students have said that they feel more refreshed when getting up early, and they have found that they have more time at their disposal. When they finish listening to the sutra lecture, it is only six o'clock, so they have plenty of time to prepare for their school work. Moreover, they can concentrate better because their minds are sharp and clear. They also feel at ease, so they are less irritated. This program enables the students to adopt a regular routine and make good use of their time.

This is what the Sutra of Innumerable Meanings describes as: "When the mind is still and free of desires, then deluded thoughts cannot enter." This is the state of mind that we pursue. Everyone should support and encourage one another to reach this goal. In this pursuit, there is no obstruction of space or time.

● **Vacation or Cultivation?**

In today's society, much importance is placed upon leisure and relaxation, and holidays are numerous. But Tzu Chi volunteers take advantage of these holidays to serve others. While other people take two days off per week, Tzu Chi volunteers use those two days for self-cultivation by doing recycling or volunteer work in the community. In serving humanity, they enhance the value of their life.

Taking the weekend to cultivate does not mean continuing to bicker and quibble throughout the workweek, and doing good only on the weekend. It would be tiring to spend two days per week on spiritual cultivation, while bickering through the other five. We should open our hearts every day, be compassionate towards those in hardship and relieve their suffering. Only when we understand the truth of life through giving and are willing to give of ourselves, our material goods, and our time, can we be truly content and at ease.

Many years ago, I met a professor who wanted to contribute his talents and experiences to Taiwan. He returned from the United States and was appointed as administrator of a hospital. At the hospital, he devoted himself fully to overseeing all operations. His wife said to me, "My husband works at least fourteen hours a day." I replied happily, "I finally found a bosom friend." It is not easy to find someone willing to use his life to the fullest. Nowadays people complain about their work hours, and always ask to work less. With this kind of mentality, how can we expect our society to grow and flourish? If everyone was like this professor, devoting himself wholeheartedly to his ideas and dreams regardless of how much time it took, then society would have a promising future indeed.

Whenever there is a long weekend, some young people will

come to say goodbye to me. I often ask how many days they plan to be away. One man answered, "Four or five days. I am going home to help my mother clean the house." I was very pleased to hear that he wanted to use his free time to relieve the burden of his parents. On the other hand, there are those who think that because they have worked hard all week, they should take advantage of the holidays to relax and enjoy themselves. This is due to a slightly deviant mindset.

We often hear people say, "We rest so that we may be able to embark on a longer journey." This seems reasonable. But we must walk forward in order to reach our goals in life. If we dwell on resting, then we become like the hare in the fable "The Tortoise and the Hare." Although the hare could run faster, he rested in the middle of the race. Eventually, he lost the race to the tortoise. Although the tortoise walked slowly, he steadily took one step at a time and finally reached the finish line.

Our life goals can be lofty, but we should never place our hopes solely in our heads. Instead, we should place them firmly on the path before us. By seizing time and following principles, we can approach them one step at a time.

Section Three – The Length, Width, and Depth of Life

Most people yearn for longevity, wealth, and well-behaved offspring. But life is impermanent; we cannot always obtain what we wish for. Nobody can predict the length of one's life, but each individual can expand the width, height, and depth of his life. If we live merely for our own sake, selfishly seeking comfort and luxury, then our life will be narrow and lonely, no matter how long it lasts.

Therefore we must broaden our life's path. The wider the path, the more people can walk with us. When our hearts are big enough to hold the universe, our love will intermingle. This is how we broaden our life.

● The Privilege to Use Life

In 2009, Typhoon Morakot and the floods that followed devastated Taiwan, destroying homes and property. Numerous people lost their lives. Many lost their homes. Nonstop torrential downpours caused mudslides and rockslides; many villagers had no time to escape. The deluge brought a huge amount of mud and boulders that buried two-story buildings in seconds. It was a terrifying sight.

Many survivors were either separated from or lost their loved ones. The grief and pain surely stayed in their hearts forever. I heard a tragic story about an old man: as August 8th was Father's Day in Taiwan, his sons, daughters-in-law, and grandchildren all came from the city to celebrate Father's Day with him. They had not even begun to eat dinner when the mudslides hit. The entire family of more than ten members was killed, leaving only the old man. In the blink of an eye their house and farmland was gone, and the whole family was buried underneath the mud. What an enormous tragedy!

What existed yesterday exists no more today. Life is indeed impermanent. I often say, *we do not have ownership of our life, only the privilege to use it.* While we are still able to exercise that right, if we uphold the correct principles and devote ourselves to serving people and benefiting humankind, we are making good use of our life. On the other hand, no matter how high our social status, if we deviate too far in our principles, indulging in wanton luxury, our wealth eventually will be used up and our fame and status will be lost if we do not seize the opportunity to create blessings. Not only will our lives end in misery, we will also have created much bad karma for ourselves.

Nothing in life can really belong to us permanently. However, if we can spread great love and serve others with enthusiasm and compassion, our wisdom-life will continue to grow forever.

In Buddhism, there is the story of two practitioners looking for a distinguished master. They went out walking for many days, and the journey became difficult. One of them said, "I am exhausted and can no longer walk. I want to stop here. I do not feel like walking anymore."

The other encouraged him, "We must be diligent in our spiritual practice. We have already walked so far in these few days. It is not much farther now. Let us continue."

"I really do not care to walk. I would rather go back and continue the cultivation on my own," the first practitioner replied.

The diligent practitioner said, "Let me do my best to help you. I will carry the heavy bags and do the tough work. But let us travel together."

The first practitioner was still contemplating whether he should accept the offer. The diligent one spoke again, "But there are a few things I cannot do for you."

"Like what?" The other asked.

"Like eating, dressing, and walking. You must do these by yourself. I cannot do them for you."

Upon hearing this, the first practitioner suddenly woke up. He thought to himself, "Yes, I must eat to fill my own stomach, and I must walk to reach my destiny. If I do not eat, I will starve to death. If I do not cultivate diligently, my wisdom-life will not grow. Therefore, I should pick up my belongings and continue on the journey."

This story teaches us to be always vigilant and to live our life carefully. If we fail to seize every moment to cultivate spirituality, our wisdom-life will not grow. As you sow, so shall you reap: no cultivation, no enlightenment.

● **Writing a Wonderful Story**

Every day is a blank sheet of paper. Everything we do is written on that paper. Wasting the day away is like scribbling and doodling on the paper, turning it into trash. On the other hand, if we use each day wisely, brilliant articles will be written and become memorable pages of history. How do we write a successful life story? By making good use of time, of course.

Mr. Chen is a Tzu Chi volunteer who is living his life to its fullest. He came to Taiwan with the army at a very young age. It was a hard time for him indeed. Accidentally injured in field training, he was discharged from military service early. After that, he worked aboard cargo ships for more than twenty years. Then he quit and became a sanitation worker. He also got married and had children.

Mr. Chen has a big heart and a strong sense of responsibility. Not only does he love his family and children, he loves every person on Earth. Being kind and compassionate, he cannot bear to see people suffer. Even though he has to work hard to make a living, he is always willing to help those in need and donate his hard-earned money.

After the 1999 earthquake, Mr. Chen devoted himself to Tzu Chi's Project Hope, a construction project rebuilding schools destroyed by the earthquake. He never missed a day of work. Sometimes other Tzu Chi volunteers did not assign him any work because they did not want to tire him out at his age. Mr. Chen thought: if they do not assign me work, I will find work myself. He called up many people to plead for the chance to contribute. He understood that others withheld work from him because they cared about him, not because they looked down on him. Therefore he actively looked for work assignments.

He thinks that doing Tzu Chi's work is a great joy and time should not be wasted, so when people told him they were concerned he worked too hard, he would say, "I am not afraid of work, I am only afraid of not having enough time to do it. Our Master has said, 'We must not put off doing good deeds or being filial.'" Each time someone mentioned filial piety, Mr. Chen became emotional.

Due to the chaotic political climate of the 1940s, Mr. Chen

left his home in mainland China at a very young age, leaving his parents behind. Time and space had prevented him from taking care of his parents as a filial son. Now he feels he must use every opportunity to do good deeds. He is determined to do all he can to contribute to society and protect Mother Earth.

Although close to eighty, Mr. Chen never wastes a moment of his time. He cares for his family, for others, and for the environment, and he has signed up to be a body donor. He also encouraged his children to be organ or body donors. From robust youth to fragile old age, he has always made prudent use of his time. What a worthwhile life he leads!

From the program "Grassroots Bodhi" on Da Ai television station, I also saw an old woman, Mrs. Amai, who is fit and healthy and takes brisk walks every day. Her children and grandchildren are all very filial. Her son often tells her that she should simply enjoy her old age and not work. But she would rather dedicate herself to recycling. She tells her son, "Recycling enables me to stay healthy and worry-free."

Mrs. Amai started farming with her adoptive father when she was seventeen or eighteen years old. She still weeds the fields even today. When she puts on her bamboo hat and covers herself with a scarf, she stands straight and tall, not a bit weaker than a thirty- or forty-year-old man. She rides her fifty-year-old bicycle out every day to collect recyclables, piling them up high on her bicycle. Her neighbors often sing her praises: "She is amazing! Even though she is in her eighties, she never slows down. She's always carrying that recycling."

She also picks up discarded bags off the street and washes them in an irrigation ditch, then lays them out in her yard to dry in the sun, before delivering them to the recycling station. A Tzu Chi staff member once asked her why she was so meticulous.

"We should be mindful of everything we do. This too is a kind of piety," she replied.

Again, she was asked, "At your age, don't you feel tired after doing so much? Don't you want to rest?"

"Of course I feel tired. I have worked quite a long time, from eighteen past eighty. You can calculate for me how many years that is. Since I am still able to work, each day is a bonus."

Let us examine the life of this old woman. How much has she contributed by effectively using her time? She has farmed all her life to provide food for people. Let us assume that there are two harvests per year. In sixty years, that is one hundred and twenty harvests. How much grain has been harvested, and how many people have been fed? She has devoted herself to her family, raised her children and grandchildren. Now she does recycling work to protect Mother Earth. Not wasting a single day in her life: that is the value of life.

Part Two — **Space**

There is love in everyone's heart. But if we love only those closest to us, then our love is too constrained. We must expand the space of our love.

Chapter 4 - Penetrating Space

Space encompasses the four directions and the opposing positions of up and down. Let us take Hualien for example. To its east is the ocean, and east of this ocean is the United States. East of the United States is another east. Because the Earth is round, there are an infinite number of easts, wests, souths, and norths. The universe is so immense and wide that it has no boundaries. This is space.

The minds of sages are not limited to the space on Earth, but are vast enough to encompass the entire universe. The Buddha's mind encompasses the entire vast Dharma-realm. One day, Maudgalyayana—one of the Buddha's top disciples, famous for his ability in supernatural powers—decided to measure the size of the Buddha's Dharma-body. He rose up and up until he reached Tráyastrimśa Heaven and then Tushita Heaven, but he still did not reach the limits of the Buddha's Dharma-body. To some people, this story is only a myth. Actually, it is an allegory to show that the Buddha's mind is so vast it can reach anywhere. Where Buddha's mind exists, the Dharma exists.

The Buddha was born in India more than two thousand years ago. After attaining Buddhahood, He travelled along the Ganges River teaching the Dharma. In that era, it was quite a challenge for the Buddha to spread the Dharma alone. It took the work of many people for the Buddha's Dharma to spread widely. Thanks to the ancient sages for going on pilgrimages to obtain the Buddhist scriptures, and for translating and teaching them. Because of their contributions, the Dharma became prevalent and continues to exist today. That is why, although the Buddha never visited Taiwan, Buddhist Dharma still prevails here. Among others, the Venerable Master Yin Shun, a great teacher of Humanistic Buddhism, transcribed the essence of Buddhism into many books. Yet more people are still needed to practice and promote Buddhism in the world.

Space is vast. No one can travel all paths in this world. Spreading the Dharma far and wide requires many people working together with great love. When everyone takes the Buddha's teachings to heart, their pure and bright thoughts can illuminate all corners. Only then can Buddhism be practiced throughout the world.

Section 1 – The Myth of Big and Small

The Earth is a macrocosm, and our bodies are like microcosms. The Earth is composed of four elements, as are our bodies. In the universe, the Earth has four elements: its hard solid shell is earth; the hot interior, which gives rise to the magnificent lava and thermal heat, is fire; the flowing waterways are water; and the air is wind. If any one of these elements is out of accord, the Earth will encounter problems.

Our bodies are like microcosms. The solid parts of the body, including muscles and bones, are the earth element. Body fluids, blood, and saliva are water. The body's warmth is fire, and our breath the wind. If any one of these elements is not in harmony, we become sick. The breathing problem of asthma, for example, is a case of the wind element out of balance. When we catch a cold and develop fevers or chills, the fire element is out of balance. People are often rushed to the emergency room with acute abdominal pains, due to severe constipation, which is the water element out of balance. External injuries and bone fractures that we see frequently are examples of the earth element out of balance. When we fall ill, we suffer unspeakable pain.

Macrocosm and microcosm are intimately related to one another. As it cycles through four seasons, the macrocosm gives life to humans and all sentient beings. Each living being is a microcosm, and there are already more than seven billion people on earth. If afflictions of greed, anger, and ignorance continue to rise because our minds are out of balance, then we will continue to commit wrongdoings and damage the macrocosm, bringing the earth into discord. The consequences will be severe indeed.

● Greed and Narrow-mindedness

Our thoughts are constantly arising and vanishing. A momentary thought can be good or bad. When an arising thought is good, we should take hold of that moment to do good deeds. On the other hand, when an arising thought is bad, we must immediately stamp it out.

Imagine if we simply allowed our bad tempers to go unchecked every time we had conflicts with others. With more than seven billion people in the world, all those bad tempers and bad attitudes would aggregate in the macrocosm. When the body's immune system is just a little weak, it can lead to many health problems. When the macrocosm consists of so many microcosms out of balance, how can it not become ill?

There is so much strife and struggle in our world. Does it not all come from greed? Why are we so greedy? Life is impermanent. We should be content and grateful to live in peace. How much more do we need to feel like we have enough? A clean and stable place to shelter us from the wind and rain is really all we need.

Our desires are insatiable. No matter how much enjoyment or wealth we have, it is never enough. Some people already live in abundance, but they long for a more luxurious life. Even if they already live in a grand mansion, they are not content, so they toil for more. How can they be truly happy?

Many years ago a Chinese woman from the Philippines came to visit me. I commented, "Your home must be very lively with so many workers there."

"I am very lonely," she replied.

"There are so many people in your house. How can you be lonely?" I asked.

She told me, "Because the house is so large, I dare not live alone. That is why I hired more servants. Some maids cook, some do the laundry, some clean the house. They all have their separate jobs."

I said, "You are the only one living there. Do you really need so many maids?"

She answered, "The labor is so cheap. I only need to provide them with three meals a day."

I said, "With so many people eating together, your meal time must be very lively."

"No, I eat alone," she told me.

"Do they not work for their three meals? Why do you eat alone?"

"They can only eat after I finish my meal and leave the dinner table," she replied.

I asked again, "Why?"

"That is their rule," she replied.

"There is no such thing as 'their rule.' You can let them eat with you. Won't you have more company then?"

"It is probably a rule between master and servant," she said.

Why is there such a big difference between the master and the servant? Maids work hard to serve their masters, yet it is so difficult for the masters to give a little bit more to their maids. How much harder it must be for them to give to a complete stranger. Some people are wealthy and live comfortably, yet they are unwilling to give a little to the poor and help them through hard times. Having so much yet not knowing how to use it, their wealth is the same as trash. With insatiable desire burning in their hearts, they are bound tightly by a rope, unable to squirm free.

Helping others is a precious blessing. When we help others we are also helping ourselves. Unfortunately, most people do not understand this principle. They do not realize that if they *give without seeking anything in return*, they can be worry-free and at ease. Therefore, people who are too stingy to give will not be able to develop respectable and lovable virtues.

I heard a story about an elderly real estate tycoon who sent his children abroad for advanced study. After finishing school, they all stayed abroad to find jobs and raise their own families. He and his wife stayed in Taiwan by themselves. After his wife passed away he lived alone. Although he owned a lot of property and assets, no one really cared about him because he had neglected to give love and friendship to others when he was young. He became very lonely. He later moved to Hualien and bought a fancy villa. Although his house was furnished extravagantly, he still lived all by himself.

In his old age, he had no one to care for him when he got sick. In and out of the hospital, he was always alone. None of his children came back to look after him since they all lived abroad. His relatives and friends also kept their distance. He finally realized that his loneliness was due to his lack of giving. With that realization, he vowed to do his best to contribute after regaining health. Unfortunately he passed away before he had the chance to carry out his vows. One day he suffered an asthma attack and died alone at home. It was too late to revive him when he was found and taken to the hospital.

So lonely he left this world. Who was there by his side? Who was there to care for him? Who accompanied him on his final journey? Who would manage his assets and distribute them? He no longer had any say in this. He did not even have the chance to fulfill his last wish. All his life, he was probably never truly happy. What could he take with him when he died? Only regrets and afflictions.

It is better to expand the cottage of the mind than to live unfulfilled in a large mansion. Once you broaden your heart, you will naturally use your money to benefit humankind, instead of wasting it lavishly. Once you change your mindset, you will be empowered to help and create good affinities with others.

● **Broad Mind, Broad World**

I often say *it is better to have a big heart than a big house.* Living in this world, if we maintain a mindset of contentment and fewer desires, then we will feel happy in any situation we encounter. Having a broad mind or a big heart has nothing to do with being rich or poor. Even if you are poor on the outside, if you have a big heart your world will be expansive.

In China, Guizhou has a beautiful landscape. Sadly, the land is fruitless, the locals are poor, and the mountainous roads are hard to travel. Some of the children must climb mountains to attend school. They get up before dawn at four o'clock every morning, prepare their own breakfast, then rush to school. They arrive at school around eight o'clock. It takes four hours of walking each way. Therefore, by the time they get home it is nine o'clock at night.

During the holidays, these students have to take cows out to the pasture for their families. Once, a Da Ai Television reporter went to Guizhou on an assignment. He saw three children sitting on rocks by the roadside and reading their books attentively. He asked why they were sitting there. The children told him that they were tending cows.

"Where are the cows?" the reporter asked.

The children looked around and could not see their cows. They were surprised to find that the cows had wandered far down the pasture. They immediately went and retrieved their cows, wearing innocent smiles on their faces.

These young kids get up so early and come home so late every day to attend school. Since their families are poor, they eat cold rice porridge and cold dishes, yet they appreciate their parents' hard work. They help out with household chores and study diligently. They live happily and are optimistic towards their future. This is being content with no greedy desires.

We often have insatiable desires, but how much is enough? No one really knows. Regardless of how much we possess, everything will be gone when a disaster hits. In recent years, California has seen many forest fires. These fires not only destroyed forests, they also burned down many luxury homes.

It is said that wealth adorns the house but virtue adorns the individual. The wealthy decorate their houses lavishly, yet individuals show virtue through conduct. If we let our behavior go unchecked and let our mind go astray, then we will need a great deal of time to bring our mind back on track. Therefore, we must always look into our hearts, eliminate greed, and dignify our minds.

There is a poor family that lives on the top of a hill in Miaoli. The parents are divorced and the father works in another city, so the three children live alone with their grandmother. Although the oldest sister is young, she is quite mature. She takes care of her grandmother and does all the household chores. She also studies hard, loves her siblings and helps them do well in school.

One day she accidentally scalded her feet with boiling water. Not able to afford medical attention, she walked with difficulty and often hurt herself. When Tzu Chi volunteers visited her family and saw the shabby housing, they decided to fix up the family's lodging first. When the girl and her father were away from home, the volunteers came to repair the damaged areas and repaint the entire house. They also added a few pieces of second-hand furniture.

Upon returning home, the girl was pleasantly surprised to see their house renovated with additional furniture. She made a vow to study harder so she could attend college and give back to society. She wanted to love others the same way she had been loved.

The girl was so strong and resilient that she had never once complained about her injury. Tzu Chi volunteers arranged for her to be treated and undergo surgery at Buddhist Tzu Chi General

Hospital in Dalin. Throughout her stay in the hospital, her younger sister frequently came and cared for her. It was touching to see the close bond between the two sisters.

There are many fortunate children who are loved and pampered by their parents. Yet they are disagreeable with their siblings and complain that their parents love their siblings more. To command the attention of their parents, they even commit wrongdoings to upset their parents. We should learn to cultivate our virtues, take good care of our loving hearts, and understand that the world will be broader when we take one step back. Only then will we be able to love others. Keep a broad mind and love and accommodate others, then we will always be loved.

In our daily lives we should nurture ourselves to be generous and giving. When we are content and have few desires, we can encompass all. With a broad mind, our world too will be broad.

Section 2 – Between Near and Far

Many people enjoy travelling all over the world to see beautiful landscapes, historical sites, and exotic places. Although I have never set foot outside Taiwan, people often tell me of the wondrous places around the world. One day someone told me that the largest and most beautiful waterfall in the world is Niagara Falls, and that its crashing waters and majestic beauty were worth seeing in person.

I said, "You have to travel all the way to the border of the United States and Canada to see it, but we can see the same thing right here at Jing Si Abode." There is a big rock with a hole in our yard. We placed some small stones in the hole to create tiers. Then we channeled water to come down from the top of the rock through the tiers of stones into an urn below the rock. We can hear the babbling and gurgling sounds of water as it flows down. A staff member took a photograph of it. Zooming in, our small waterfall appears as magnificent as a big waterfall. Without getting on an airplane or spending so much time, we can see this beautiful scene right here in our own yard. Because we use our hearts to see and feel, when our hearts are beautiful, whatever we see will be beautiful.

The scenery within each person's heart is prettier than any scenery outside. Traveling overseas is a complicated process; one must rely on many modes of transportation to arrive at the destination. Even when the landscapes are breathtaking, how long can you stay there to admire them? You still need to return home. No matter how beautiful the view, it is temporary; you cannot enjoy it for long.

● The Distance of Thoughts

When the Buddha was traveling through the land of Sravasti he told his disciples, "There are a myriad of phenomena in this world, yet none can change faster than the mind. There is also nothing that the mind cannot imitate. For this reason, we must take good care of our minds. As soon as a bad thought arises, it must be suppressed immediately and carefully. If we keep close watch over our own minds, then the principle of all things lies within."

Many people have seen the peony flower. If you ask them what a peony looks like, the image of the flower will appear in their minds right away. Even if it is not the season for peony, the flowers will bloom in their minds. Is this not an example of the fast transformation of our minds?

Or if you ask people how to write the number '1', everyone can produce it very quickly, although not everyone can write it neatly. Those who can write it properly must have taken the time to practice writing it. However, our minds can immediately produce a beautifully written '1'. Even when it comes to complicated strokes, our minds can still imitate or manifest the writing quickly.

In addition, our thoughts can transform quickly. No matter how far the physical distance, our minds can arrive at any location instantly. Argentina is very far from Taiwan. It takes more than thirty hours to fly there. But as soon as the country is mentioned, images of my Argentinean disciples doing volunteer work immediately appear in my mind. I have never been to Argentina, but I have seen the pictures and video clips of their Tzu Chi activities, so there are images of Argentina in my mind.

Intangible thoughts can overcome tangible distances. A few years ago, Malaysia experienced its worst flooding in a century. When the local Tzu Chi volunteers called me to report the situation, they told me that the rain was pouring down nonstop. Everyone was worried about the Tzu Chi office being flooded, so they all went to move the objects upstairs.

At that time, my physical body was in Taiwan but my mind had reached Malaysia. I expressed my gratitude to the local volunteers for their vigilance in the disaster relief effort. At the same time, I was worried about whether the disaster area would expand, and when the heavy rain would stop.

While on the phone with volunteers in Malaysia, I received another call from China's Fujian Province. They wondered whether they should distribute relief supplies of food and comforters the following morning as planned, even though the quality of the rice was different from that in the contract. I said to them, "Please discuss this carefully with the team. If you cannot distribute the rice as scheduled, you must inform those coming to receive it. If you decide to distribute it, then you must use your wisdom to tactfully handle the situation."

After I hung up the phone, I realized that my consciousness had traveled far and my mind had shifted quickly. In the course of a few minutes, my mind traveled from Taiwan to Malaysia, and as I picked up the other phone call, it had gone to mainland China.

How far can our consciousness expand? I believe it is limitless. Tzu Chi started from a borrowed space in Puming Temple, and then moved to Jing Si Abode after its construction in 1969. From this location, we gradually expanded our physical space to every corner of Taiwan. Later we extended gradually overseas and proliferated across all continents. In this world, wherever there are people there is love. Although I have never been to any of those countries, as long as our hearts and our missions are in unity, I know that Tzu Chi volunteers everywhere are with me every day and I with them, no matter how far those countries are. The most remote area feels like it is just next door; no matter how far or wide the physical distance, our hearts are always close.

● **Space of the Mind**

Modern technology enables us to measure the size of the earth, yet we are still unable to determine the size of the universe. We feel that the earth we inhabit is enormous. Are humans large? In fact, we are quite insignificant. Nonetheless, the Buddha teaches us that our minds are vast enough to embrace the universe. If our hearts are pure and free of affliction and obstruction, then we will not cause harm or commit evil; the world will be at peace and the earth will revolve safely along its orbit.

Our hearts are the same as the Buddha's. The Buddha's heart is as vast as the universe, but our hearts are filled with limitless desires that create pollution and lead to disasters. When the world is filled with desires, it is in danger.

In recent years, global warming and climate anomalies have become serious problems, causing frequent disasters. The earth's environment has reached a critical condition. Therefore, everyone on earth needs to do good and create blessings. The accrued love and blessings will form a benevolent atmosphere of harmony to fill the universe and safeguard the earth like a protective shield.

As the universe is immense, our love must spread far and wide. It is essential that everyone has a big heart and acts with kindness and virtue in order to take the initiative and use our abilities to help others. There are so many suffering people in the world. When one Tzu Chi volunteer sees a person suffering, it is like a thousand Tzu Chi volunteers have seen it. More people can see more places. Wherever Tzu Chi volunteers are, compassionate eyes will be looking at sentient beings. With everybody helping in concert, no matter how filthy or damaged the environment is, it will become beautiful again. With their boundless love and openness of heart, they cannot bear to see people suffer. They see others as their own family and take care of others' soiled environment as their own.

When those who suffer come out of misery and smile, then they feel happy too.

If you ask me how long I want to live, I will say, "I do not know." Yet, if you ask, "How broad is your loving heart?" then I will reply, "My heart can reach to every corner of the world." For instance, for a time there were frequent news reports of conflicts in the Gaza Strip. Even though the United Nations worked hard to mediate, there was no sign of an end to the violence. It was truly worrisome.

We have a close affinity with Israel. The famous Israeli singer and musician David D'Or has come to Taiwan on charity concert tours for Tzu Chi. He has even translated some Tzu Chi songs into English and Hebrew. In 2008, Tzu Chi took on the relief effort to help the disaster victims from the cyclone in Myanmar and the earthquake in Sichuan. To lighten Tzu Chi's load, David volunteered to give a charity concert tour in the United States, and donated all the proceeds to Tzu Chi for disaster relief. David and his band members are all young musicians. They tour around the world to perform in concerts. David usually wears a large beard, but he shaves it off each time he comes to see me to show his respect. He later took refuge with me as my disciple, and has even placed a prayer for my health in the Wailing Wall in Jerusalem.

During that period of violence and unrest, I was very concerned about the situation in Middle East. Whenever I went to Taipei,

Raphael Gamzou, the Israeli Representative to Taiwan, would come to tell me that everything was fine. Mr. Gamzou knew that I was worried about David's well-being, so he relayed a message his wife sent from Israel which said that a recent bombing was still fifteen miles from their home. So he asked me not to worry. I thought to myself that fifteen miles is not that far. It was still quite dangerous, and I heard that even internationally-banned white phosphorus bombs were used. In the footage on TV, I saw many children in panic and mothers fleeing with children in their arms. The suffering was unspeakable.

Not long after that, David called to tell me that he decided to move from Gaza to the countryside. He felt deeply for those panicking children, so he led them in singing to ease their fear and worry.

Israel is far from Taiwan. But there is no distance between caring hearts, especially with today's technology. Da Ai TV has allowed us to see happenings from around the world and to care about worldly affairs. From the news media, for example, we learned that the provinces of Inner Mongolia, Qinghai, and Heilongjiang in northern China had suffered heavy snows in the early fall. These snows toppled trees and power lines and damaged houses. They made us realize that abnormal climate change is really happening.

On Da Ai Television, I also saw Tzu Chi volunteers in Islamic countries using their free time on holidays to do Tzu Chi work. Malaysian volunteers distributed food and daily necessities to the poor during Eid al-Fitr, a holiday much like the Chinese Lunar New Year, so that the poor may enjoy a bountiful holiday. The majority of Jordanians are Muslims as well. There are only a few Tzu Chi volunteers there, but they have been caring for the Bedouins in the desert for a long time. In order to give a few hundred Bedouin families a happy Eid al-Fitr, they drove through dust and wind for eight hours roundtrip to deliver relief goods. They also passed out school supplies and schoolbags to the children to facilitate their studies.

No matter where they are, Tzu Chi volunteers around the globe make good use of their time. They diligently put Buddhism into action and mindfully walk the Bodhisattva path. They enter deeply into their communities to find out exactly what is needed. Tzu Chi volunteers make practical contributions with diligence and love. Their hearts are broad and open, so the space that their love inhabits is naturally broadened.

Section 3 - The Pull of the Heart

Buddhists believe that all sentient beings have a shared karma. Karma means action. The power of collective karma should not be taken lightly. The more people there are committing wrongdoings, the stronger and more powerful the evil forces. When the pull of evil is strong, it is very likely to trigger disasters and karmic retributions.

Karma is like an air current. A typhoon is also a kind of air current. If high pressure is strong enough to suppress low pressure, a typhoon will change its course. All of us should do more good acts, speak more kind words, and think more good thoughts to bring forth the power of blessing. A little virtue and blessing can overcome a disaster; much virtue and blessing can eliminate disasters. Therefore, the more good people there are doing good deeds, the more blessings will flourish. When blessings flourish, they bring forth good fortune.

In our modern world, we need to gather together much good fortune to make the Earth healthy, society harmonious, and climate favorable. Yet the only way to gather good fortune is through love. When we inspire people to love, good fortune is increased with every loving heart.

● Transforming the Environment with our Minds

When we are discontent, it is easy for our minds to fill with hate. No matter the surrounding environment, the mind is of the utmost importance. If we look around, we see that although some people are rich, they always feel something lacking, as if they can never satisfy their desires. When people are unhappy, they tend to have more afflictions and attract more troubles to entrap themselves. If people are content, they feel grateful. With a grateful heart, their hearts are open and their minds are pure. They can then use their hearts to transform their surroundings.

Mr. Zhang grew up in a dysfunctional family. Not long after his birth, his family began to move constantly to escape creditors. More than ten years later, his family's financial situation improved a little due to his father's hard work. But his father was irresponsible to his family, and before Mr. Zhang entered the army, his father wrote bad checks in his mother's name. As a result, Mr. Zhang's mother was saddled with the debt and incarcerated. Mr. Zhang's displeasure toward his father turned to hatred.

While serving in the military, Mr. Zhang missed his mother terribly, so he deserted. He was constantly on the run. He joined a gang and was eventually captured. Imprisoned for many years, he was nearly forty years old when released. One can only imagine his pain of spending the prime of his life in darkness.

Despite his many transgressions, Mr. Zhang remained filial to his mother. After being released from jail, he and his mother lived together on her government stipend, barely making ends meet. He encountered great difficulty in finding a job. When he did find work as a doorman for a building, he had to leave because he fought with a colleague. Due to the adversities in his life and his work, Mr. Zhang thought of taking his own life. Luckily his mother detected his intentions and anxiously asked Tzu Chi for help. Tzu Chi volunteers felt great sympathy when they heard what Mr. Zhang had gone through. They organized a family care group to visit him at his house. Seeing the family living in such a shabby place, Tzu Chi volunteers decided to help.

After getting the Zhangs back on their feet, the volunteers frequently invited them to the Tzu Chi Dongda Campus in Taichung, and encouraged them to volunteer in the recycling center. Mr. Zhang witnessed a volunteer in the final stage of spinal cancer who came to the campus everyday to garden, water the vegetables, and do recycling. Although stiff in his movements, this volunteer had shown up every day since he was diagnosed with the disease three years earlier. He did not waste a minute or a second of his time.

Mr. Zhang realized the importance of cherishing his life. Originally he planned to ask Tzu Chi to take care of his mother and walk away. After seeing the other volunteer cherish his life so dearly while dying of cancer, he began to understand that *we do not have ownership of our life, only the privilege to use it.* He became a Tzu Chi volunteer, and accompanied his mother in doing recycling work. Now he has a steady job in a restaurant and lives a peaceful life with his mother. He has even become a member of Tzu Chi's Tzu Cheng Faith Corps. Through these experiences, his life has been profoundly transformed.

Mr. Zhang said that Tzu Chi volunteers are so committed to recycling, they pick up even a small piece of wasted paper for the sake of protecting the earth. Though he felt that his own life had been a waste, Tzu Chi was able to recycle him and make him into a useful person. This testifies that "when you change your state of mind, the environment is changed, too." Once you have set your heart to overcome challenges, there is nothing that cannot be overcome. When you turn your mind toward virtue, life will be peaceful.

This same mother and son used to have a hard life. Mr. Zhang was trapped in a dark place and could not come out. Now, by changing his perspective, he is living a stable life. His heart is filled with love, so he is able to help others even though he is still not well-off. Once we have a positive thought, our mind changes accordingly and the environment transforms, too. When we face everything with a positive attitude, we forgo our hatred and embrace love instead. In doing so, we liberate ourselves from the darkness, and our lives become bright and beautiful.

The Buddha said, "The mind alone creates all." When an individual shifts his perspective toward doing good and applies that virtue to everything, then nothing is difficult to handle. Similarly, we can apply this principle to the whole Earth and its abnormal climate and frequent natural disasters. These can all be mitigated if everyone maintains a virtuous mind. In fact, global warming originated in people's minds. When our minds are out of balance, our tempers are unstable and our dispositions are discordant. We easily commit wrongdoings, create bad karma, and damage the earth. How can we expect the weather to be favorable?

If everyone maintains a love that is selfless, harmonious, and pure, then an effect will come into being. We should not take this effect lightly because the power generated from its chain reaction can influence the entire human race. In science, there is the butterfly effect. Though a butterfly is an insignificant insect, the slight flutter of its wings can cause giant waves. How much more powerful an effect would our hearts generate!

No matter where we live, we must all take on the human mission and become seeds of love. The Sutra of Innumerable Meanings states, "One gives rise to infinity, infinity begins with one." Our love can expand from one seed and develop into myriad seeds of love. When we combine the love of everyone, we can work together to establish a loving environment. As long as we reduce our greed and desires, refrain from indulging in pleasures, and show respect to one another, we can make our world a pure land.

● The Tug-of-War between Good and Evil

There is a proverb, "A single good deed eliminates one thousand disasters." This does not mean that when we do good deeds, we will not get sick or suffer from disasters. All sentient beings have a shared karma, and the entire universe is always engaged in a tug-of-war between good and evil. A place with more benevolence will have fewer disasters, and a place with more evil will have more disasters.

In a tug-of-war, the side with more people will have more strength and is more likely to win. Therefore, a region with more good people will be more peaceful; even when disasters happen, the suffering will be less. Confucius said, "How can he be considered wise who does not choose to dwell in moral surroundings?" This advises us to carefully choose the place in which we live. We should select a place with many virtuous people for, as Confucius said, "It is the moral character of a neighborhood that constitutes its excellence." Indeed, a place with more virtuous and moral people is the most beautiful place, and choosing to reside in that place is a wise choice.

How do we make a place into a village of virtuous people? When many good people encourage each other, their numbers will grow. When everyone does good deeds, the effect will start: from one hand to one hundred hands to one thousand hands, and eventually to an infinite number of hands. These hands will be able to help the needy and save those who are deluded. Typhoon Morakot is a good illustration of this. In August 2009, after the typhoon hit southern Taiwan, numerous Tzu Chi volunteers went to the disaster area to help clean the homes of the victims. Because the area was covered in mud, volunteers had difficulty walking there, let alone carrying heavy buckets full of mud. But with so many people eager to help, volunteers formed a long line and passed buckets of mud down the line. When everyone works in unison, damaged homes can be rebuilt.

One volunteer was always very dedicated in videotaping Tzu Chi's activities for the purpose of keeping history. When his house was flooded, the one thing he thought of rescuing was his video camera. Though water had not receded from his own home, he immediately joined the disaster relief effort to document the events. His story was quite touching. None of the Tzu Chi volunteers complained, "I'm doing Tzu Chi volunteer work. How come my house is also flooded?"

This is because good karma did not triumph over bad karma. To eradicate disasters in the world, we must inspire everyone to nurture a good heart and encourage people to do good deeds. When we emphasize good, not evil, and positively influence one another, the power of benevolence will increase.

A good or bad surrounding has an even greater influence on the individual. At one of the Tzu Chi General Hospitals, a volunteer once discovered that a middle school student had a gun in his schoolbag. The volunteer quickly approached the student to ask why he carried a gun. The student replied frankly that it was a toy gun. Sensing the boy's behavior was going astray, the volunteer wanted to counsel him. He asked the boy about his family and his school. The boy was candid and told the volunteer that his school was full of violence. He left home to live in a rented apartment. He even told the volunteer that he was a gang leader and that he could collect protection money.

The volunteer was worried about the boy's ignorance. Patiently he told the boy many stories, such as the criminals he had seen at the hospital wearing foot shackles and handcuffs. It was too late to feel sorry then; they would live in remorse for the rest of their lives. The boy felt that the volunteer really loved and cared about him, so he took his advice to heart. The volunteer told him, "You must change your ways. In a tug-of-war between good and evil, a good friend will give you a helping hand but a bad friend will drag you down. Come to see me whenever you have a question or are confused."

From then on, the boy called the volunteer when he ran into problems. Sometimes he went to see the volunteer in person. Two years later, the boy invited the volunteer to his graduation ceremony. The volunteer was very touched when the boy was honored as a model student.

After the ceremony, the volunteer asked the boy about his plans. He said that he already found a job and wanted to work for a while. The volunteer said, "Working is good, of course. One has the chance to excel in any profession. But I am afraid that you may be dragged down again."

The boy replied, "Never, because there are now benefactors in my life. Once you told me about the tug-of-war between good and evil. I have so many Tzu Chi volunteers behind me, supporting me. I am confident that I can take care of myself." He also admitted that members of his old gang still contacted him often, but he had changed his cell phone number and was focused on being a good person.

Other than the power of benevolence given him by Tzu Chi volunteers, whenever he felt confused and alone, he would read Jing Si Aphorisms. This was also a positive influence for him, so he felt confident about himself.

A kind word can influence people positively. Our campaign Good Words Fill the Streets has received much support from taxi drivers and tour bus operators who post Jing Si Aphorisms in their cabs and buses and take these good words anywhere they go. Tzu Chi volunteers from different communities have shared many touching stories about this campaign. They said that many people have been changed by these *Jing Si Aphorisms*. Many became friendlier to one another because they began to speak kind words, and ceased fighting and competing with others. As they became more humble, their world became more spacious, too. How beautiful this kind of society is!

Not only are good and evil locked in a tug-of-war, calamity and blessing are as well. Wrongdoings create calamity, and good deeds create blessing. We need more people doing good deeds to create more blessings. Everyone is a farmer tilling the field of blessing. We must work hard to spread the seeds of love, so that there will be more living Bodhisattvas.

● A Good Environment Inspires Virtue

After the 1999 earthquake in Taiwan, we took on the challenge of rebuilding fifty schools, an endeavor called Project Hope. One entrepreneur at that time wanted to cover the entire cost of rebuilding one specific school. But Tzu Chi commissioners suggested that he create affinities with more people: by not specifying the school on which to spend his money, he would be participating in the reconstruction of all the schools. He gladly accepted the proposition and donated his money to Project Hope.

This exemplifies the act of taking from society, then giving back to society. When we profit from society, we should give back to society when needed. Nowadays many entrepreneurs and people in society have already turned their thoughts to altruism. If more people can be called to do good deeds, the power of benevolence will be even greater.

Project Hope is not only about rebuilding schools but also making school campuses beautiful. As education should develop students' character and morality in addition to knowledge, the school itself should provide a positive learning environment so that as soon as students and teachers enter the school, their hearts and spirits can be softened and beautified by the environment.

We built the schools with attentiveness and dedication. All the buildings were made sturdy and earthquake-resistant so that these schools will withstand the passage of time. They were made to be functional and attractive even after a hundred years, like works of art to brighten up their surroundings. Over the course of two years, fifty schools were completed one after another, like fine works of art emerging from the rubble.

I have heard so many touching stories about these schools. I remember once I was traveling in central Taiwan and took a detour, as I often do, to visit a school. The school had just let out for the day, so I decided to get out and walk around for a little bit. Some administrators were still at work. One of them accompanied me on a walk around the school's central courtyard. As we passed the sports field, I saw students playing sports there. It was gratifying to see students willing to stay at school after classes had ended.

I also heard one of the principals say that his students asked whether they could stay at school after class. It is certainly the result of a positive learning environment when students are willing to stay long after the school day ends.

In addition to the buildings, there are many intangible qualities associated with a school. More than a decade has passed since the earthquake. Many principals from these fifty schools have said to me, "Master, our students have been doing very well since the school was built." The earthquake has released the love of the public to provide students with a positive learning environment. Principals and teachers have also changed their attitude in teaching. The students were all happy to learn. Those who were in primary school at the time are now in college. Many of them have become Tzu Chi collegiate volunteers.

In 2008, when a major earthquake struck China's Sichuan Province on May 12, we in Taiwan were as shocked as those in mainland China. Taiwanese businessmen in mainland China immediately mobilized and traveled to the disaster areas in Sichuan. Two days later, Tzu Chi volunteers from Taiwan also arrived. They immediately took action to comfort survivors and provide them with hot meals. They also involved locals to volunteer for their own communities.

When emergency relief ended and Tzu Chi volunteers took leave of Sichuan, they left behind the spirit of volunteerism. Their volunteer work was kept alive by local volunteers and a group of local youths who took over the job of caring for seniors. When Tzu Chi volunteers returned to Sichuan after some time, they were pleased to see that the locals now live a stable life and that the seeds of volunteerism have taken root, so the Tzu Chi volunteers began to teach them recycling. When the Luoshui community center was complete, it became a recycling station for collecting and sorting recyclables.

Those living in temporary housing have never severed their connection with Tzu Chi. They have participated in discussion groups to learn how to apply Buddhism in their daily lives. They have come to understand that everyone can be a living Bodhisattva and help others. Although they used to have bad habits such as playing mahjong, drinking, and smoking, they were willing to quit them all in order to become Tzu Chi volunteers and adhere to Tzu Chi's ten precepts.

One elder commented, "I am very happy to do Tzu Chi work. I enjoy sorting recyclables. I am especially pleased to know that plastic bottles can be used to make eco-friendly blankets. We can help people and help Mother Nature at the same time!" He made a vow to quit gambling.

Everyone knew that he was a man of his word, so they encouraged him to go further: "Will you make a vow to quit smoking and drinking as well?"

He said that this was a difficult task, but many people encouraged him to make one more vow.

"All right, I will not drink for two days a week."

Everyone gave him a round of applause and asked him to quit smoking as well.

"This is extremely difficult," he said.

"How about quitting for one day a week?"

He yielded under everyone's encouragement. "All right. I will not drink two days out of the week, and not smoke one day out of the week."

After a period of time, since he went to the recycling station every day, he did not have any chance to drink. He lived each day happily and his mind was clear. Eventually he quit smoking, drinking, and gambling altogether. His wife said that his temper had changed too. His story shows that it really is not difficult for an ordinary person to become a Bodhisattva.

All in all, we can see that the influence of our environment is very strong. To develop one's love is to spread the seeds of love. When everyone has love in their hearts, then this love will become the force of virtue.

Chapter 5 - The Measure of Happiness

Back when Tzu Chi was just founded, my disciples and I lived in a hut borrowed from Puming Temple. Three years later, Jing Si Abode was built. At that time, it was only the main hall. During the day, we worked and practiced spiritual cultivation in the hall. At night, we pulled the sliding door closed and the hall became our place of rest.

Even though space was limited, that very winter we set up fifteen tables outside by the lotus pond and hosted a hot pot dinner for some poor and lonely elderly people. As the years passed, modern technology now allows us to see the whole world from Taiwan. There are Tzu Chi volunteers in seventy countries on six continents. Volunteers in more than ten countries are able to hold video conferences with us in Taiwan. Although we are separated by time differences, the love we all possess is exactly the same. This is how our space is broadened.

These spaces are reached as Tzu Chi volunteers pave the way with love. Every individual has a loving heart. By inspiring and encouraging one another, we can expand our love to every corner of the world. This is what it means to have a heart that can encompass the universe.

Section 1 - A Drop of Water and the Ocean

In recent years, we have been encouraging people to "Return to the Bamboo Bank Era." We urge each person not to underestimate his or her own abilities. Small contributions can be combined to make a significant difference. Before each disaster relief distribution, we explain to recipients that the relief materials were donated by kind-hearted people all over the globe. By giving whatever we can, our donations are like drops of water merging into the sea: together we can help many people. We also encourage recipients to create more blessings by helping others.

When they receive relief materials, recipients also take home bamboo banks to save money that can help the needy. For example, in Dreamland Muzon, a poor seaside village in the Philippines, the residents all live in shabby houses. When typhoons hit and the sea level rises, their houses are all flooded or destroyed. Their village is also home to the municipal garbage dump site. The children live and play near the dirty garbage dump all day. Their parents cannot afford to send them to school, so they are unable to escape poverty when they grow up. Is this not a vicious cycle?

Tzu Chi volunteers have taken care of the locals here for many years. Not only do they provide material aid, but more importantly they have opened the villagers' hearts to feel the joy of helping others. The villagers have started to each save just five or ten centavos (less than one US penny) per day: a small amount that does not affect their daily lives. Before long, they filled two large earthen jars with coins. This shows *that many drops of water make a river and many grains of rice make a bushel.*

This village now has more than three hundred Tzu Chi members who are empowered to help those who suffer. When we put our minds to it, we can guide and nurture the poor to have love in their hearts: like lotus flowers emerging from the mud one after another, full of hope.

● Like Nanotechnology: Small in Size, Great in Strength

If we are selfish and only care about our own profit, we are bound to worry about gains and losses, and our lives will be full of suffering. Only when we humble ourselves and devote ourselves to helping others can our lives be all-embracing.

A few years ago, Pakistan was severely damaged by a strong earthquake, so Dr. Qiu Conglang of Hualien Tzu Chi General Hospital went there to provide free clinics to survivors. His son, then in the sixth grade, strongly supported his virtuous act of saving lives. The boy worked hard to assemble a small lamp equipped with a generator. He gave it to his father and insisted that he take it with him to Pakistan. So as not to disappoint his son, Dr. Qiu took the lamp to the disaster area, and used it the very first night to illuminate the darkness.

Pakistanis are not directly related to us, yet the world is all one family. Even though the country was far away and the people foreign to us, we treated them as our own family. Dr. Qiu and his son utilized their abilities to help others because they have big hearts; they care for everyone in the world. Every person, young or old, has this innate goodness. We should not belittle ourselves or look down on others, but rather believe that our love is selfless. If we can be selfless, then we will have immense strength to help others. However, we should not think "nothing can get done without me," but rather "I should contribute what I can to every good deed."

As spiritual practitioners, we should be humble and shrink ourselves to the size of specks of dust. Only then are we worthy of love. If we inflate ourselves to the point of being rude and abusive to others, others may consider us unapproachable. As such, even if we have a multitude of talents, we are confined to ourselves. And the power of one individual is limited.

To live a life as humble as dust, we should first be gentle. Just as Confucius was gentle, kind, courteous, restrained, and tolerant, so must we be gentle and kind, and treat everyone with gratitude and humility. Only then can we bring to life "the power of nanotechnology."

In this modern era we have nanotechnology, a field that deals with objects on such a tiny scale that they are almost invisible, yet their function is mighty. The state of mind that we maintain should also be like nanotechnology: miniscule yet powerful, yielding the full scope of respect and great love. So how can we minimize our interactions and behavior to the size of nanotechnology? We must be polite and modest. In other words, we must show respect for others and minimize our egos. We will be able to forgive others and embrace all only when we are respectful and show our great love.

There is a young doctor in the Tzu Chi International Medical Association (TIMA) who was an accomplished nephrologist in the United States. During one of his trips to Taiwan, he took advantage of some free time to volunteer at Tzu Chi General Hospital. Since he looked very young, he was mistaken for a Tzu Chi collegiate volunteer by a few members of the Tzu Cheng Faith Corps. They assigned him to push sickbeds, give patients baths, and empty bed pans in the Emergency Room.

This doctor did not reveal his identity. Instead, he worked joyfully with a selfless spirit. Shrinking himself and letting go of his ego, he worked cooperatively with other volunteers in perfect harmony. Later, when people learned that he was a well-known attending physician, they all deeply admired and respected him. A person with no attachment to ego, status, or fame is truly respectable.

We should all learn to be as humble as dust while making

as great an impact as nanotechnology. Then we can truly put Buddhism into action. When we inflate ourselves, we become an eyesore to others, and it is hard to be accepted and welcomed. Only by humbling ourselves can we enter others' hearts.

● **One Person versus Sixty People**

Each of us has a "self." If we are too attached to this "self," then we tend to be egocentric and deluded, and we will eventually create bad karma. We must constantly reflect on ourselves to examine whether we are lost or if we clearly understand the truth, whether we have changed from a selfish individual to a selfless person or to an arrogant person.

Some may wonder, why talk about "self" when our goal is the state of "selflessness"? This is because most people are prejudiced about the "self," so we must first understand the true meaning of "self." If people take responsibility for themselves, for their families, for their communities, and for society, so that the whole society is harmonious and free from disasters, then we will be blessed and each individual will be at peace. Extending the limited love of an individual to a great love for the entire world is what the Buddha called "great enlightenment."

The early days of the Tzu Chi Foundation are known as the Bamboo Bank Era because the foundation began with thirty housewives each saving two pennies every day. Before they went out to buy groceries, they put two cents aside from their grocery money to use as charity funds. In the market, they told the vegetable vendors that they wanted to buy a bit less to save money.

"What good is it to save such a small amount of money?" the vendors asked. They replied that even this small amount of money could save lives. Once the vendors understood the idea that *many drops of water make a river, and many grains of rice make a bushel*, they donated money as well. The idea of one individual inspired good thoughts from thirty people, and every day they created blessings and kept spreading good thoughts to inspire more people.

More than forty years later, we are still holding on to the idea of that moment, an idea that has never diminished in the slightest. Beginning with just a handful of people at the outset, the cycle of love and goodness continues to repeat with more and more. It only takes a second for an individual to make a vow, but what can a single individual accomplish with his or her limited power? It is too trivial to mention. However, with ten individuals, there are ten seconds and ten times the power. With sixty individuals, the time and space expand accordingly. Imagine how much space expands with six hundred people and six hundred seconds! It is not easy for one individual to save a person, but if sixty people extend their helping hands together, it is not difficult at all.

With effort, anything is possible, so we should not be afraid of difficulties. From its founding place of Hualien, Tzu Chi Foundation has spread near and far. The seeds of love have spread to many countries around the globe. For instance, Tzu Chi USA was established by Mr. Huang Siyuan and his wife Li Jingnian who were immigrants in the United States. During one of their return trips to Taiwan, they learned about Tzu Chi and decided to introduce the spirit of Tzu Chi to the U.S. to relieve suffering with compassion.

During one of his visits to the Jing Si Abode, Mr. Huang asked me, "Master, can we develop Tzu Chi in the U.S. with our limited resources and manpower?"

I told him, "The greater the resolve, the greater the blessing; the bigger the vow, the stronger the power. As long as you are sincere about spreading the spirit of Tzu Chi in U.S., you will have the power."

Mr. Huang replied, "I'm sincere."

The couple worked diligently to promote Tzu Chi and inspired many people there. An American lawyer was so moved by Taiwan Tzu Chi's relief efforts that he decided to help register Tzu Chi with the U.S. government. Thus, Tzu Chi USA was formally established.

Later, Mr. Stephen Huang purchased a clinic as the Tzu Chi

office. Tzu Chi volunteers began to spread Buddhism and carry out Tzu Chi's missions. By doing so, they cultivated both blessings and wisdom. In addition to helping the poor and inspiring the wealthy, volunteers held free clinics every month. Many Taiwanese doctors either donated money or personally participated in the free clinics. More and more people joined in to carry out the Tzu Chi missions, and they were all happy doing so.

The Tzu Chi chapter in Japan was also started by a Taiwanese immigrant. During one of his trips to visit relatives in Taiwan, the man met a Tzu Chi commissioner and was delighted to learn about Tzu Chi. He came to visit me in Hualien, and vowed to carry Tzu Chi to Japan with his own resources.

When he came back to see me again, he told me that sixty or seventy people had joined in to do Tzu Chi work in the first month. I said to him, "I only had thirty members in the beginning, but you had sixty or seventy people in the first month. Your influence is indeed great!"

So, as long as we are mindful, we can inspire more people to be compassionate. We need to remind people to open up their hearts and not underestimate the strength of each individual. Even when we start in just one location, if each person can influence another, the gathered strength will be enough to spread kind thoughts far and wide.

Section 2 - From Dots to Lines to Planes

Many years ago, I had a conversation with an elder in southern Taiwan that I still remember vividly. The elder said to me, "Master, I have a feeling that Tzu Chi will one day become the largest family in the world."

I asked him what made him think so. He said, "Because Tzu Chi's heart is very big and its love is truly great. You live in Hualien, yet when disaster strikes southern Taiwan, you come here immediately to help the victims as if they were your own family. With this mindset, I believe that all of Taiwan will be one big Tzu Chi family."

When we unite with one heart, get along harmoniously, love one another, and work together in concert, all volunteers are as one family. We should treat everyone in the world like family members, love all living beings, and contribute selflessly. If we expand and broaden our love not only in Taiwan but across the world, then is it not true that the entire world is one big family?

● Take from the Community and Give Back to the Community

With the convenience of modern travel, many Taiwanese have moved abroad to develop their businesses. Quite a few of them had already joined Tzu Chi before they left and wanted to maintain this love for Tzu Chi. Some of them told me before their departure, "Master, I can leave everything behind but I must take with me the seeds of Tzu Chi." They vowed to sow Tzu Chi's seeds wherever they went.

I always advised them, "When you develop your business in a foreign land, you employ local workers and use local resources, so you must give back to the community. And as the old saying goes, "Better a neighbor nearby than a relative far away." You should create good affinities with the locals. Take the initiative to love them and make them feel that you are friendly and approachable, then you will be loved." They took my advice to heart and put it into practice. Gradually they have spread Tzu Chi's great love all over the world.

Many people who do Tzu Chi work outside of Taiwan follow this principal: they take from the community and give back to the community. They raise funds locally and do charitable works locally. For instance, Tzu Chi volunteers in the Philippines often provide free clinics to remote or impoverished areas. For more than ten years, they have helped many needy people by relieving their suffering.

There was a cataract patient who had not been able to see clearly for a long time. At one of the free clinics, he underwent surgery. The next day, after the doctor removed the gauze from his eyes, he was so happy to have regained eyesight that he said,

"I want to announce to all Filipinos that Chinese people are very good to us. They help us. Please do not rob or kidnap the Chinese." At that time, the Philippines had many social problems due to economic and social disparity. There had been many cases of Chinese being kidnapped. Therefore, helping others is in fact helping and protecting oneself. When we love others, others will naturally love us in return.

Once a Tzu Chi volunteer called me from South Africa and said, "Master, I have decided to close my factory here."

I asked, "Why do you want to close the factory when your business is doing well?"

He replied, "Robberies and arsons are frequent in South Africa; it is difficult to keep the factory operating."

Racial confrontation in South Africa had existed for a long time, and riots broke out quite often during that period of time. Local people did not like Chinese, so many Chinese were robbed and their houses were set on fire.

I said, "Why were they robbed? Why were their houses set on fire? It was because those people took advantage of the local labor and resources but enjoyed the profit by themselves. The local workers had been earning low wages for a long time. They lived in poverty and felt that they had been treated unfairly, so they reacted with violence. If those merchants could not only take from the community, but also give back to the community by giving workers reasonable benefits and making local living standards more balanced, then their own lives would become more secure.

I also told him a true story that had happened in the United States. A Tzu Chi member emigrated to the United States from Kaohsiung, Taiwan, and started a bakery business. The city he lived in was mired in racial riots at the time. One day he drove his car to deliver bread downtown, when he was suddenly stopped by a group of armed African-American rioters. They asked him, "Are you Japanese or Korean?"

He replied in fear, "I am Taiwanese."

The group changed their attitude right away. They told him gently to avoid downtown and showed him a safe route to quickly drive home.

The Tzu Chi member was curious about the incident, so upon returning to his store he asked a female African-American employee why he was spared. She told him, "We are grateful to the Taiwanese for improving our lives and helping with our children's education by providing scholarships, so we all agreed not to attack or rob Taiwanese."

He asked, "Who are the Taiwanese that have helped you?"

She replied, "Tzu Chi. Tzu Chi people from Taiwan helped us."

The man was so pleased to hear this that he quickly called his friend in Taiwan who was a Tzu Chi commissioner. He said, "I am calling you today to thank you because Tzu Chi USA saved my life. In the past, I thought that donating money was to help others, but I learned today that it was also to help myself. I will continue to donate."

Tzu Chi volunteers in the United States raise money locally to help local underprivileged people. They contribute to the locals under the name Taiwan Buddhist Tzu Chi Foundation. Because of that, the locals not only recognize Tzu Chi but also Taiwan. This is a testimony of how we benefit from the love we give.

After hearing this story, the Tzu Chi commissioner in South Africa said to me, "I know what I should do." From then on, he worked hard to introduce Tzu Chi and its spirit to Taiwanese businessmen there. He also started to help and care for the locals and influenced the locals to volunteer with Tzu Chi and pass on that love and care.

● Taking a Journey of Ten Thousand Miles

A proverb states, "Traveling ten thousand miles is better than reading ten thousand books." Each year we hold an event where participants jog from Hualien Tzu Chi General Hospital to the Jing Si Abode. The sight of people jogging always reminds me that if people do not move their feet forward, they will never reach the Jing Si Abode. Once we set our goal, we must move forward. However much time we spend advancing forward, that is how far we will go, and how much we will see.

In January 2002, Indonesia was hit by several days of continuous downpour. Jakarta was flooded and the Angke River did not recede for more than a month. Jakarta is the country's capital and economic center, and is surrounded by many poverty-stricken communities. The flooding was so severe, how could the people in these communities carry on with their lives?

Old Mr. Huang, a successful entrepreneur in Jakarta, came to Taiwan to see me. I told him, "If the flood water does not recede for a long time, there will be sanitation problems. Infectious diseases may spread which affect not just the poor. The consequences will be unimaginable. The rich should take care of the poor. Those who are able should extend a helping hand to the flood victims. We must support one another in this world."

Mr. Huang was compassionate and felt the same way. He was willing to provide help but did not know how to do it. I proposed a five-part plan: pumping out water, cleaning up the disaster area, sanitizing the area, holding free clinics, and building a Great Love Village.

While assessing the damage and caring for the victims, we had to pump out the water as quickly as possible and clean up the area.

These two things needed to be done at the same time because it would be more difficult to clean up after the area had dried out, but doing both concurrently required a great many people. As Mr. Huang was a very influential figure in Indonesia, I asked him to call on the government to dispatch soldiers and policemen and mobilize local residents to do it together. Sanitizing the environment and providing free clinics then followed to prevent infectious diseases.

Since this area was prone to flooding every time there were heavy rains, the long-term solution was to demolish all the illegally constructed buildings along the river and to dredge out the mud and garbage from the river.

The illegal constructions along the river had existed for a long time. Since it was not easy to make a living in rural villages, many villagers had come to look for work in the capital city. Unfortunately, many could not land jobs and ended up homeless. Little by little, these people came to settle along the Angke River. The river had been seventy meters wide but was reduced to a mere ten meters due to illegal construction, increased population, and the dumping of garbage. The environment had become extremely dirty, leaving the river choked with garbage, and this overloaded river lead to frequent flooding in the area.

Understanding the problem, Tzu Chi volunteers in Jakarta decided to dredge the river. Not only did they finish the first four parts of the five-part plan within two weeks, they also actively went out and looked for land to build permanent housing for the displaced residents. With assistance and support from the local government, a parcel of land on the outskirts of the capital was allocated for a Great Love Village. In order to dismantle the shantytown, the government subsidized rental costs for residents and persuaded them to move away from the riverbanks. The government was able to instill confidence in them to accept the moving arrangement.

As soon as the Great Love Village was constructed, these people started to move into their beautiful new homes. Indonesian Tzu Chi volunteers also set up job training centers in the village to provide villagers with skills with which they could make a living, such as sewing and cooking. The volunteers also taught them to recycle, and the villagers began to make and sell doormats of discarded carpets. In doing so, not only was discarded material reused, the residents' lives were improved as well.

In addition to homes and job skills, education was vital. A Tzu Chi primary school and high school were built in the Great Love Village. These schools taught good manners to the local children, transforming them into little ladies and gentlemen. As these children participated in various competitions, they began to rack up numerous achievements. It is hard to imagine that in only three short years, the villagers' living situation had changed so dramatically.

A few years later, Tzu Chi high school teachers in Taiwan took their students to Indonesia for a cultural exchange. Many students already knew the story of the Angke River, but even though they had seen video clips of the filthy environment and barefoot children with runny noses and shabby clothing, the Taiwanese children remained skeptical. "Is it real?" they asked. "Are there really people still living like this in today's world?"

Since dredging the Angke River was such a mammoth project, it had been implemented in phases, so some shanty houses were still standing at that time. The teachers decided to take their students to the Angke River to experience the filthy environment and the life of the children they had seen in the video. The students also visited the newly built Great Love Village.

The village students attending Tzu Chi schools wore neat uniforms like their counterparts from Taiwan, and they also studied hard in school. During the visit, each of the local students hosted one Tzu Chi student from Taiwan. The Taiwanese students interacted with their host families to experience local culture and customs. They witnessed a piece of history and saw with their own eyes the transformation of these poor children.

The Angke River story shows that with good karma and blessings, we have an opportunity to change destiny.

Section 3 - Love Transcends Distance

The Buddha treated all sentient beings as his own children and showed compassion for all. We should learn to be as big-hearted as the Buddha, take the Buddha's heart as our heart, and care for all suffering beings in the world regardless of race, religion or nationality. We should love all the Earth's creatures.

I saw a news report that said that the rate of ice melt and glacier collapse in the North and South Poles was faster and much more serious than previously thought. The Arctic and Antarctic regions are so far away from us, do these happenings really have anything to do with Taiwan? Yes, they do. In fact, they are closely linked with us. Since the island of Taiwan is small, it will be greatly affected by climate change and rising sea levels.

Actually, everything in the world coexists with the earth. Therefore, we need continuous great love in this world. When everyone in the world has a heart so big as to encompass all, the distance between people will be decreased and hearts will become fonder toward one another.

● The Ripple Effect of Great Love

Love is the secret to wealth. How can we possess everything in life? By opening our hearts and not insisting on possessing things. We should learn to embrace the mentality that "when others are well-off, I feel rich." In other words, when other people own wealth, it is as satisfying as when we own it ourselves.

Many years ago, when we were raising funds to build the first Tzu Chi hospital, I met with many rich ladies. I would often hear them comparing the size of the diamonds on their hands and the value of their jewelry. I asked them, "Why do you demand that your husband buy you a large diamond when you see that someone else has a bigger one? There is no end to comparison. If you simply admire the diamond ring on someone else's finger, you will feel no burden at not having one yourself."

The pursuit of material things is endless. We should learn how to become rich with compassion.

Da Ai TV reporters once produced a feature on students in Gansu Province, China. Although they were lacking in material things, these students were very content. Though they had but a primitive school to attend, they felt they were richer than others; they were grateful and satisfied even if they had to walk several hours to school each day. At the school, the reporters saw a student tightly grabbing a one-centimeter pencil with her fingertips. Even though she could write only with great difficulty, she was happy to have the lead to write with because materials were so scarce there.

The reporters were deeply moved. After returning to Taiwan, they initiated the "Blessings from a Pencil Case" campaign, which was enthusiastically received. In a short period of time, people donated more than twenty thousand pencil cases filled with pencils, ballpoint pens, and colored pencils. Twenty thousand loving hearts were like ripples spreading out to create a cycle of love. The donated stationery was delivered not only to Gansu, but also to Afghanistan, Nepal, and other countries short of supplies.

A child's tiny pencil brought forth the love of more than twenty thousand people. It shortened the distance between Taiwan and Gansu, and even between Taiwan and Afghanistan and Nepal.

How much of a ripple effect can stem from a single good thought? No one knows. Once Tzu Chi International Medical Association (TIMA) volunteer doctors in the Philippines held a free clinic in Zamboanga. A patient suddenly vomited, and a Tzu Chi volunteer nearby caught it with his bare hands, just as a mother would do for her own child. Witnessing this, a Catholic man was so moved that he joined Tzu Chi. A stranger's action had brought forth his love; he began to help people and brought great benefit to the locals.

Ms. Xie, who immigrated to San Diego, California, from Hong Kong, is another example. She often traveled to Mexico on business and discovered a group of Mexicans living without documentation in the border town of La Morita. These people came from all over Mexico with the intention of smuggling themselves into the United States. But that was not easy to do, so they ended up living in poverty in the village.

La Morita is a desert town without water or electricity. The living conditions are truly very difficult. Ms. Xie felt sorry for the local people, so she brought their case to the attention of Tzu Chi USA. Tzu Chi International Medical Association (TIMA) began to provide free clinics in La Morita, and Tzu Chi volunteers gradually reached out to the locals to further understand their needs. In addition to providing medical care, medicine, and supplies, the volunteers also built a school for them, because education is necessary to give the children hope for the future.

As most parents were illiterate, they felt they had no hope themselves. But they wanted their children to have the opportunity to go to school. Tzu Chi's love and compassion also deeply influenced the school's principal and teachers, who taught the students well by incorporating Tzu Chi's humanistic culture into their lessons. Even some nearby permanent residents moved to that village so that their children could attend the Tzu Chi school.

This place that was poor and desolate gradually turned into a lively town. Tzu Chi volunteers often visited and later held courses to teach local women sewing skills with which to make a living. Not only did the town prosper, the children were well-educated and the locals' lives became stable. With peaceful and contented hearts, they no longer think of smuggling themselves into the United States.

We hope that each individual can do his or her best to inspire others and promote the power of love, no matter which country they are in. I often talk about the importance of having an effect. We should not underestimate our own strength, however weak it seems. A drop of water can trigger ever-widening ripples, and anyone can become that drop of water to initiate a ripple effect.

● Eliminate All Barriers

Selfless love should make no distinctions between people, place, and race. In the late 1990s, Afghanistan suffered from turmoil, civil war, and a devastating earthquake that killed more than five thousand people, injured many more, and left one hundred thousand homeless. At that time, we desperately wanted to help the victims, yet we had no access to enter the disaster area. Finally, we were able to connect with an international charity organization in Los Angeles. They had means to go to Afghanistan, but lacked relief goods. So Tzu Chi and this organization reached a partnership.

The disaster relief team had to enter Afghanistan through neighboring Uzbekistan because all local ground transportation and airports were closed due to civil unrest and the aftermath of the earthquake. It had snowed heavily for a few days before they departed, so the helicopter carrying the relief supplies was unable to land for some time. While circling in the air, it was almost caught in the line of sporadic gun fire.

Dr. Edward Artis was the man responsible for delivering the relief supplies. Prior to this trip, Dr. Artis was deeply moved when he learned about Tzu Chi's principles of focusing on priority areas and distributing aid directly to victims. When the flight situation became critical, he vowed to drop the relief supplies by parachute if the helicopter could not land.

When they finally landed after several attempts, Dr. Edward was so grateful that he knelt down and shouted to the sky, "Thanks to Tzu Chi Taiwan for making this extremely difficult relief possible!"

After arriving in the disaster area, the relief team was deeply moved to find that it had been part of the Silk Road two thousand years ago. One mountain had numerous Buddhist grottoes and three giant Buddha sculptures; each of them forty meters high. After the earthquake, many people had become homeless. To shield themselves from the blizzard, they went inside these Buddhist grottoes for shelter. Dr. Edward could not believe how this incredible relief mission had come together: as a Christian, he carried out the mission of a Buddhist organization to deliver relief supplies to an Islamic country. And the locals, devout Muslims, were taking refuge in Buddhist grottoes.

Everyone must respect life, and love must be open and wide. We have to unite our efforts to help those in need. Regardless of religion, race, and nationality, we should get along peacefully with one another, and contribute our love together. Only then will the world truly be at peace.

Whatever happens, we should always reflect upon ourselves. We must contribute first, then we will receive affirmation from others. There is an Islamic boarding school in Indonesia that takes in many impoverished children. Several years ago, this school of more than four thousand students asked Tzu Chi Indonesia for support, and Tzu Chi volunteers agreed to provide them fifty tons of rice every month for two years.

When the term of assistance was nearing its end, the executive director and deputy executive director at the Tzu Chi Indonesia office informed me that the imam of the boarding school had asked Tzu Chi to support the school for one more year. I said to them, "We can support them for one more year. However, many students at the boarding school are young adults, the oldest are eighteen years old. They are strong and healthy; you should teach them to become self-sufficient."

The imam was compassionate and took in many young students, so the government gave the school a piece of land about one hundred and fifty acres. The land was not used for anything special, so the volunteers suggested to the imam that he should plant crops on it. The imam agreed wholeheartedly. With the help of Tzu Chi volunteers, the students began to till the land to plant rice, corn, wheat, and vegetables. The students even learned to make flour and bread from the wheat they harvested.

Now the students are able to grow crops on their own, and they have also learned to do recycling. The school is grateful to Tzu Chi, which they see as another kind of spiritual education. Therefore, they hold a class each day in which the students read Jing Si Aphorisms. In addition, three thousand students were assigned to receive Tzu Chi volunteer training and now joyfully carry out volunteer work.

When people are inspired to have great love, they see that all sentient beings are equal. All the religions of the world preach love, and we should love and respect one another.

In September 2009, several typhoons ravaged the Philippines and caused severe flooding that affected several million residents. The flooded areas were covered in trash and mud. If left that way, infectious diseases could soon break out. Since it was impossible for local Tzu Chi volunteers to clean such a large area alone and local residents had no income after the flooding, Tzu Chi came up with a cash-for-work program that enlisted local residents to clean up their own communities.

The local government endorsed this program because of its many benefits. More and more residents joined the program: first a few hundred, then a few thousand, and finally more than ten thousand. Tzu Chi volunteers not only paid them wages respectfully, but also provided hot meals. The love shown by the compassionate Tzu Chi volunteers moved many local residents into action because they had experienced first-hand the power of love.

Despite the mud and filth, the locals participated actively in the cleanup and worked side-by-side with Tzu Chi volunteers. To them, it was not a job but a mission to clean up their own community. Their hearts opened.

One resident said, "My house was covered in garbage and mud. The thought of cleaning it all by myself discouraged me. With the cash-for-work program, I get paid every day and there are many of us working together. I'm happy even when I clean other people's houses. And my house got cleaned today!"

After cleaning up their own communities, some residents volunteered to work in other areas. They said, "We're volunteers today. We don't want compensation." Tzu Chi volunteers wisely guided and encouraged the locals to love and help one another. The more people there are, the more they can accomplish, and more people elsewhere can benefit as well. To express their gratitude to Tzu Chi, the locals collected money and made a banner that read, "Special Thanks to Taiwan Tzu Chi." Holding the banner in their hands, they marched down the streets they had cleaned themselves. It was indeed heart-warming.

We all live under the same sky and tread the same earth;

why should we make any distinction between peoples, races, or nationalities? If we all possess the same great love and work together to help all sentient beings, then this world will truly become a Pure Land.

Part Three — Interpersonal Relationships

When we all do our part and show respect to each other, then all people will love one another. If we are all determined to walk the path of virtue, then society will be in harmony and the world will be free from disasters.

Chapter 6 - Initiate the Cycle of Love

If we always receive love from others, then it will be hard for us to realize the joy of giving. Because we are accustomed to receive, we will think, "I deserve it," and not be appreciative. If we are without gratitude, we hold no respect toward others and cannot have intimate relationships with other people. So how can we give love sincerely?

There is a story about two groups of people sitting at two round tables loaded with delicious food. Each person has a pair of long chopsticks. At one table, people scramble for food, but the chopsticks are too long to deliver food to their mouths. Whenever they see other people reach for food with chopsticks, they get anxious, upset, and suspicious. Their minds, disturbed by greed, are not at peace. Anger leads to confrontation, so they start to throw bowls at each other until the table is overturned and all the delicious food is destroyed.

At the other table, even though the people hold the same long chopsticks, they are able to help and love one another. Each person delivers food to the person sitting across the table. In this way, they can all enjoy the cuisine. The people in this group are thankful toward one another. They live happily as if in heaven. Although the living conditions are the same, their different attitude makes the outcome totally different.

Section 1 - Begin with the Mind

Sometimes people sigh and complain that everything is so difficult. Where is the difficulty? It is in the mind. Our minds differentiate between likes and dislikes. We are drawn to the things we love, and are prejudiced against the things we dislike. As a result, our minds are tormented. When we cannot move past the situations we encounter, we feel that everything is difficult.

Actually, many things are quite simple, and it is not time or space that pose obstacles. As long as we are determined, we can turn a narrow bumpy road into a smooth thoroughfare. The Buddha teaches us that we must begin our spiritual cultivation by taking care of our minds. If we cannot discipline our minds, we cannot cultivate ourselves. Once we take good care of our minds, no road is impassable.

● Train the Mind to Be Simple

Sometimes things in the world puzzle us. What appears simple can actually be very complicated. Let us look at people. The Chinese word for person is 人 (ren). As a character it is very simple—only two easy strokes—but it can be very difficult to understand. There are three types of people: lovable people, pitiable people, and detestable people. The world is full of these three types of people, and love, pity, and hatred are all afflictions of complication. These two simple strokes refer to three different types of people, each of which is very complex. Isn't this a perfect example of simplicity becoming complicated?

The affliction of complication is the same as ignorance. When external conditions do not gratify us, our temper and habitual tendencies flare up. Although we clearly know that we must control ourselves, we are unable to tame our hearts.

Once, at a medical exhibit in Jing Si Hall, a director of psychiatry showed me a specimen of a brain biopsy. "We still do not know how thoughts and consciousness are formed, but we can use brain biopsies to analyze the brain. For example, this area controls emotions," he explained, pointing to different grain patterns on the biopsy specimen. Looking at it, I thought, "Isn't this the source of affliction? Our lives are complicated because we are unable to control our emotions, and because we each have habitual tendencies."

Actually, these nerves, like muscles, can be trained. The Buddha said that each person has the same wisdom and pure nature as the Buddha himself. Through spiritual cultivation, we can bring out our innate kind nature, control our emotions, and rectify our habitual tendencies.

All sentient beings often make simple matters complicated, but we should conduct ourselves with a simple mindset, and refrain from cunning and trickery. For example, when someone asks whether you have eaten, you can answer "No, I haven't" or "Yes, I have" in a straightforward manner, and then thank them for their concern. When you respond simply, both parties feel warm and friendly.

But some people may think, "Why did he ask me whether I have eaten? Does he think that I have difficulty feeding myself?" When we twist another's words and make them complicated, we misunderstand their intentions. A simple matter becomes complicated when viewed with a complicated mindset. On the other hand, everything becomes simple when we treat it with a simple mindset.

Granny Aduan has been a simple person all her life, as she was born intellectually challenged. She begged for food with her parents until she was almost twenty years old, then her parents and stepparents passed away one after another. She was left homeless and alone. Her fellow villagers found her a deserted house and cleaned it up so she could live there. Although Aduan could not even speak clearly, the villagers had known her for a long time and knew that she was kind and diligent. They often asked her to babysit when they were busy, and found that she was very careful and mindful when taking care of their children.

Ever since she was young, Aduan has helped people with a simple mindset. Almost every villager has sought out her help, and many children have been under her care at one time or another. Although she is now old and alone, she is like a family member to the whole village. When she gets sick, she is treated by the village doctor free of charge. Some villagers even leave cash at the grocery store regularly so that Aduan may take home the items she needs. She is not greedy; she only takes what she truly needs. She is indeed a person with a great heart and a simple mindset, and is content with few desires.

Later in her life, Granny Aduan became a Tzu Chi recycling volunteer. People sometimes ask her, "You collect recyclables; do you know what the money is used for after they are sold?" She always answers cheerfully, "Sell. Tzu Chi. Good." Although she can only say a few simple words, she clearly shows a pure innocence free from desires and complicated thoughts.

In Chinese, we often use the phrase "open heart" (開心) to describe the state of being joyful and worry-free. In other words, we must open our hearts to be happy. Sometimes we ask a person, "Why are you so gloomy?" He or she may answer, "I do not know. My heart seems to be tied up." When we close up our hearts, it is as if we are bound and entangled, so we naturally feel that things are complicated and difficult to resolve.

I often say, "Simplicity is beauty and purity is kindness." When we write, if we want to depict auspiciousness and perfection in one stroke, we draw a circle. It is that simple. Likewise, if we treat everything in the world with a simple mindset and loving care, everything will be perfect and beautiful. We should not become like the fluctuating, entangled line drawn on a seismograph by an earthquake. That would be most unsettling.

A simple line of perfection and an irregular, entangled line are totally different. So we must always be vigilant to maintain a simple and moderate mindset. We should not be influenced by irregular shockwaves. When we take good care of our minds, we will always be happy in whatever we do. With a simple mindset every day, we can draw a perfect circle with one stroke. Otherwise, we will face endless ignorance and affliction.

● The Most Beautiful Word

Tzu Chi volunteers often say "gan en" which means "I am grateful." When uttered from the bottom of one's heart, gan en is not only the most beautiful spoken word in the world, but also the most sincere interaction between people.

In order to tame our tempers and reduce conflict, gratitude is also needed. We should start with ourselves: every day when we wake up, the very first thing we should do is to be grateful. We should wear a smile often and express our gratitude to every family member. When we leave home, we should be grateful to our neighbors, and even to strangers that pass by.

One day, while I was traveling to Taipei, I looked out the bus window and saw a man lying on his stomach by the roadside. As I looked closer, I realized he was a worker pulling cables through a culvert. He was working hard in the scorching heat wearing waterproof plastic overalls. I turned around to tell everyone in the bus, "We should be grateful to laborers. Because of their hard work, we have smooth roads to travel on, utilities for our daily use, and sturdy houses to shelter us. All those things are accomplished by the hard work of laborers." We should say gan en to people from all walks of life for a stable society.

"Gan en" and "thank you" differ greatly in depth. Gan means to feel, and en means a great favor that one person bestows upon another. En (恩) is the combination of two characters: "cause" (因) over "heart" (心): the cause is like a karmic seed planted deep inside the heart, which then grows and flourishes to bear fruit. As such, gan en articulates a profound gratitude from deep inside one's heart.

For example, when we tell someone a wise saying, he accepts it and says "gan en." If this saying moves him, so that he keeps it inside his heart and applies it to his daily life, then it becomes Dharma. If he is truly grateful, he will plant this Dharma deep inside his heart. Only then will he be able to apply it daily. Therefore, being grateful is most essential.

We all came into this world alone, and we will leave this world with nothing but our karma. From birth to death, we all hope everything will turn out to our satisfaction. But in reality, the more desires we have and the greedier we are, the more difficult it is to have everything we want. If we are content and have fewer desires, then we feel that everything is as we desire. Contentment enables us to be grateful and appreciative.

I once saw an elderly Tzu Chi recycling volunteer carefully sorting cans and bottles. Some bottles still had leftover sauce inside. She dug it out carefully, rinsed the bottles clean, and then put them into the recycle bin. She truly cherished her blessings and valued every item. Was she tired from all this? Of course she was. But she told me, "I am grateful to have this field of blessing that allows me to make good use of my life. I would be lying if I told you I was not tired. However, my back hurts anyway even if I do nothing, so I might as well do recycling work and sleep better because of the fatigue." This woman is able to make good use of her life because she has shifted her mindset.

In addition to gratitude, people should respect one another; then their genuine love will arise. "Gratitude, respect, and love" are as simple as that. I often say, Cherishing our life is a way to repay our parents. Giving of ourselves is a way to show gratitude. We should start with ourselves to love ourselves and love others. It is our duty to cherish our own lives. It is a blessing when we respect and love others. We should always show love in our interactions with people.

● Optimism, Understanding, and Love: Three Essentials for a Healthy Mind

It is our nature to love beauty, and we are all attracted to beautiful things. There are three kinds of beauty. The first is the beauty of our environment. When we cherish our natural environment, take care of it, and maintain its cleanliness, then the environment will be pleasant and comfortable. The second is physical beauty. When we keep our bodies healthy and our appearances neat and clean, our lives will be beautiful. The third is the beauty of the mind. When our minds are diseased, then even with a healthy body we will suffer unspeakably.

How do we maintain a healthy mind? First, we must be optimistic. Second, we must be understanding. Third, we must have a loving heart. When we are optimistic and content with our lives, then our hearts are wide open. With open hearts, how can we not be understanding? Understanding people always keep their hearts open, so that they can always extend their love.

There are people who keep their hearts tightly closed and only care about themselves. This is attachment to self; this egocentricity impedes the growth of knowledge and wisdom. We should open our hearts to allow wisdom to shine within. Then we can illuminate the external environment with our inner light to bring hope and happiness to others.

There were once two sisters-in-law. The older one was always criticized by her mother-in-law after she married into the family. The younger one had a strong sense of justice and always felt that her mother was unreasonable for being sarcastic toward her sister-in-law. Each time the older sister-in-law accepted her mother-in-law's sarcasm with a smile, the younger one would say, "Why are you so stupid? Do you not understand what she means?"

The older sister-in-law would reply, "She is educating me. She pointed out my wrongdoing so that I can make corrections accordingly."

The more obedient the older sister-in-law was, the more protective the younger one became. She felt her sister-in-law really needed her protection, otherwise insult and abuse would follow.

One day the younger sister-in-law brought the older one to see me. She said, "Master, please advise my sister-in-law, as she is very foolish"

"What makes her foolish?" I asked.

"She does not understand my mother's sarcasm. She simply accepts the humiliation."

"Are you not upset at all when your mother-in-law scolds you?" I asked the older sister-in-law.

She replied, "My mother-in-law has more experience and has

seen more. When I do something wrong and mother-in-law points it out, I should correct it. The more corrections I make, the better I will become. Far from being angry, I am grateful to her."

I told the younger sister-in-law, "Your sister-in-law is a joyful person. She is not angry at all when being scolded. Instead, she is grateful for it. She is wise and very understanding. What is wrong with her being content? On the other hand, you listen to your mother's words with a different mindset. You have only grasped the bony part of her speech; you do not see the beautiful meat of her words."

Embarrassed, the younger sister-in-law said, "I see that it was I who was mistaken."

When people interact with each other, everything is relative. If one person has a worse temper or worse habits, the other one should take a step back. It is like a dance. When one person steps forward, the other one should step backward. Between advances and retreats, each person should show respect toward the other. It is important to note that when one is narrow-minded, one sees and hears things in a biased fashion. Therefore, we should learn to see things correctly in their full beauty.

A Tzu Chi commissioner often visited and cared for one of our members who suffered from depression. This member told the commissioner, "I don't know what I am worrying about. Maybe I am worried about the instability of my husband's business, or about my children's academic performance."

The commissioner said to her, "Do not worry. The Master has said, When you open your heart, your destiny will change and blessings will come."

After hearing this, the woman thought to herself, "Every day my heart seems to be bound up so tight that I often suffer from insomnia. Afraid that something bad might happen, my husband stays up at night to keep me company. I should find a way to open up my heart."

She recalled that the commissioner often invited her to volunteer at the nearby recycling center. She began to try doing recycling work. Although it made her physically tired, she was happy and forgot to worry. She slept well every night. Since her husband no longer worried about her condition, he could focus on his business. Her children were already well-behaved and did not need her to fuss over them. After a period of time, the commissioner visited her again. Upon seeing the woman, the commissioner said, "You look different. You seem to be quite at ease."

She said, "I am grateful to you. Now I do not need to take any medication. My husband can concentrate on his work, so his business is doing much better."

The commissioner asked, "How did you let go of all of your worries?"

She replied, "You told me, When you open your heart, your destiny will change and blessings will come. Realizing that worrying would not solve any problems, I decided to find a way to open up my heart. I started to do recycling work. It was enjoyable to work and interact with others. I worked diligently and forgot all my troubles."

Her story is a good example. We are ordinary people, easily troubled by our families and external disputes. We cannot completely let go of our worries, but sharing good words we have heard with others is a virtue. The fortunate people who hear and take those words to heart will be able to apply them in their lives. Those who apply them happily will eliminate their delusions, and eventually reach mental liberation.

Section 2 - We All Have Unlimited Potential

I saw a news report about a teacher who teaches visually impaired students with computers. He guides the students to experience the world with their hands to broaden their view. Although these students cannot see the beautiful landscapes in the world, they now have wonderful scenes in their minds. He is truly a good spiritual teacher for his students.

These visually impaired students have pure hearts. They do not seek materialism or long for pleasure. They are content with rich spiritual nourishment. These students have even learned to walk about freely in their own space without the help of walking sticks. It is a testimony that we all have unlimited potential.

Man is said to be the master of all living beings because human beings have wisdom. Wisdom is the most precious thing. When our wisdom is obscured by worries, we begin to rely on material enjoyment, which is empty and worthless, like a flower that quickly withers away, or a dream that vanishes as fast as sea foam. We should all return to living a practical life, so that our lives can be meaningful and valuable.

● Fulfill Our Duties, Enhance Our Abilities

One day many years ago, I was ready to give my morning teaching after our morning service. It was still dark; everything was calm and tranquil. I heard birds chirping in the trees and insects singing on the ground. I even heard the frogs croaking. I looked outside and saw a frog in the faint light. It hopped a few steps and then jumped into the lotus pond. That morning I told this story:

One morning, the monks in a Buddhist monastery were going through their morning service. The scene was solemn and dignified. During the service, a frog leapt into the main hall. Seeing the service, the frog felt envious and inferior. It thought to itself, "It is so nice to be human. They have two legs to walk on, and they are elegant and graceful when they pay their respects to the Buddha. I wish I could have two legs like the humans. The frog prayed every day, and finally his dream came true.

This frog stood up and walked on his two legs, proudly showing off how he was different from other frogs. Then a big hungry snake appeared. The other frogs quickly hopped away. Yet the frog that walked on two legs had given up its original ability; it was unable to jump away in the face of danger. At the critical moment, it regretted its action. "Why did I want to mimic humans and lose my own ability?"

This story illustrates the importance of upholding our duties. As humans, our duty is to protect all beings on Earth and create peace with light and love in our hearts.

When we uphold our duties, we also enhance our abilities. That is, when we mindfully do our best in our daily lives, we naturally gain the abilities to make a living. However, if we are envious of other people who are wealthier and higher in status, we have transgressed our duties. There are some who vigilantly uphold their duties; even though their living conditions are inferior to others, they have a natural ability to transcend themselves.

Mr. Xie Kunshan, for example, is truly remarkable. People say that "our two hands are capable of anything," but Mr. Xie has no hands. It is said that "we can travel ten thousand miles with our two legs," yet Mr. Xie is handicapped in both legs: one leg is missing, while his toes on the other atrophied due to injury. We say that "we can see everything in the world with our two eyes," but one of Mr. Xie's eyes is impaired. Nonetheless, his natural talents and his ability to make a living transcend those of ordinary people. He is very independent in his daily life. For instance, when he brushes his teeth, he puts the toothbrush on the rim of the wash basin, secures it with his short arm stub, and moves his head to brush his teeth. His teeth are white and healthy, with no trace of fillings. In addition, he is able to do housework and take care of his young children. He always thinks of new ways to make it work.

Mr. Xie has diligently studied painting. One of his works, a painting of lotus flowers, hangs in the hallway of the Heart Lotus Ward in Hualien Tzu Chi General Hospital. If you look carefully, you can see the Buddha's image embedded in the painting. Many people are not able to produce such a magnificent painting with their two hands, yet he did it by holding the paintbrush in his mouth. Not only does he earn a living with his talent, he also teaches this skill to others. He sets a great example for many people who are physically healthy but spiritually impaired.

Everyone has the natural instinct for survival. When we do not fulfill our duties, we will lose our natural instinct and abilities and be unable to behave properly. I often watch the seniors in the "Grassroots Bodhi" program on Da Ai Television. I am delighted when I hear them say something philosophical. These elders may not be well educated, but if you listen closely, there is truth in their words that comes from their life experience.

Due to the prospering economy, many families today live comfortably and children are spoiled with rich resources. Because of this overly comfortable lifestyle, they become discontented and their spirits suffer unspeakably. On the other hand, children from poor families know that they should work hard, love themselves, be content, and fulfill their duties. They live in the joy of simplicity.

In Chiayi, there are two little girls who used to take care of their paralyzed and bedridden mother so that their father could go to work. The older sister would run home from her primary school during ten-minute recesses to turn her mother over in bed, look after her hygiene, help her into a wheelchair, and then run back to school. The younger sister, a kindergartener, would help with household chores after school. The two sisters never complained about their situation and they also maintained good grades in school.

Later, Tzu Chi volunteers learned of the family's hardships. They arranged for the mother to be treated in the hospital. The sisters not only took care of her during her hospitalization, they also volunteered in the hospital. After rehabilitation, their mother can now sit in a wheelchair and move about by herself.

What qualifies as the best environment? It is an environment in which we can abide by principles, fulfill our duties, and utilize our abilities. When we encounter obstacles in life, we must immediately summon up our courage and face the obstacles responsibly. Then we will not have wasted our lives.

● Abide by the Rules, Attain Freedom

We are all pursuing something. Some seek physical freedom while others seek spiritual freedom.

There are two types of approaches in the pursuit of spiritual freedom. Some people discipline their own minds, pursue the truth, and learn to accommodate and forgive others. They try to achieve spiritual freedom by acquiring a peaceful mind. Others are more narrow-minded. They dwell on petty matters and cause disputes. They think that individual freedom means doing whatever they want. Actually, their minds are like wild horses running wild, filled with fears and afflictions. How can they attain spiritual freedom this way?

Likewise, there are two ways to pursue physical freedom. One is practiced by those who fulfill their duties, abide by principles, act cautiously, avoid wrongdoings, and dedicate themselves to helping people in need. As a result, these people are worry-free and at ease no matter where they are. Yet there are others who hold deluded thoughts. They think that they can do whatever they want. They race cars, take drugs, and indulge in excessive pleasure, which often result in the loss of their physical freedom.

Wise people pursue the true liberation of both body and mind. If we abide by the rules and at the same time benefit humankind, our bodies and minds will be joyful and at ease. We will then achieve true liberation. On the other hand, freedom without self-control is as dangerous as an ignorant child playing with fire.

On the path of life, each of us should respect other people's freedom. We should not hinder another's freedom by acting only on our own will. We cannot abandon character education and etiquette. When we all follow rules and moral principles, take on our own responsibilities, and nurture good intentions, the world will be blessed. If we stress "liberation" and "freedom" without rules or guidelines, we will lose our direction and there will be chaos.

Therefore we all must have rules and precepts in our lives. Precepts help us avoid wrongdoings, stop evil deeds, and prevent ourselves from overstepping propriety. They provide us with a code of conduct to guide our behavior. As humans, we should focus on our humanity and follow human morals. We must uphold the five precepts and five constant virtues. We must discipline ourselves to avoid wrongdoings and observe the five traditional relationships. If we can do this, then all will be good and society will be harmonious.

The five constant virtues are benevolence, righteousness, etiquette, wisdom, and trust. These five constant virtues correspond to the five Buddhist precepts: benevolence to "no killing," righteousness to "no stealing," etiquette to "no infidelity," wisdom to "no alcohol," and trust to "no lying." These constant virtues and precepts spell out the correct path in life.

The first precept is "no killing." Life is the most precious thing in the world. Killing others and killing oneself both violate the precept of "no killing." The Buddha has taught us to love and cherish all beings, as all beings share the Buddha's nature. If humans regard themselves as the masters of all beings, they must protect all the myriad beings in the universe.

The next precept is "no stealing." When an individual desires another's wealth and property and takes actions to obtain them, he or she is liable to commit a minor theft or major robbery. A robbery attempt may even lead to killing. Therefore, stealing is prohibited.

"No infidelity" is also necessary. Husband and wife should love and respect each other; that is the foundation of a happy family. If either side commits adultery, it will disturb the family and society as well.

"No alcohol": we should always keep our minds clear and sharp so that wisdom may develop. Drinking alcohol disturbs our disposition. A great number of crimes are committed because people lose their reasoning and self-control.

"No lying": we must be true and sincere in order to be respected and trusted. How can a person conduct himself in this world if he is not trustworthy? As Confucius said, "I do not know how a man who is without good faith is to get on. Like a wagon without its yoke-bar for the ox or a carriage without its collar-bar for the horses, how can these be made to go?"

The five traditional relationships are the relationships between father and son, ruler and subject, husband and wife, elder and younger siblings, and friends. These are the rules of human relationships. In today's society, the ruler-subject relationship can be viewed as the employer-employee relationship. The employer should trust the employee and the employee should be loyal to the employer. Parents and children should uphold their close relationship. Husband and wife should be polite to one another and work together to shoulder their family responsibilities, including raising children. No one should depart from these rules. In the family, older siblings should be kind to younger ones, and younger ones should respect their elders. Friends should keep their word with one another.

Upholding the etiquette of human relationships is our basic duty as human beings. The five precepts and the five traditional relationships are all fundamental rules to maintain an orderly society as well as a happy family. When each of us upholds the five cardinal relationships, abides by precepts, and carries out moral principles, we will live happily and peacefully, and our society will be harmonious and healthy.

● Self-Discipline Leads to Plenty

Mr. Lai, Assistant Superintendent of Dalin Tzu Chi General Hospital, once told an interesting story. Although short and light-hearted, it held profound truth.

A child was walking down the street. He started to cry sadly when he noticed he had lost ten dollars.

"Why are you crying, child?" a Good Samaritan asked.

"I lost ten dollars," the child replied.

"Do not cry. I will give you the money."

After receiving the ten dollars, the child cried even louder. The Good Samaritan thought that the child was moved to tears. He tried to comfort the child, "Do not cry. It is only ten dollars, not much."

The child replied, "I am crying because I would have had twenty dollars now if I had not lost my ten dollars."

Most people have the same mindset as this child. Of course we are sad when we lose something. But are we happy when we regain our loss? If we are not content, then we will never be happy. I often say that many people are "having one, lacking nine." For instance, people with high salaries often begrudge a little extra work: they complain about lacking overtime pay, extra allowance on business trips, and so on. These people get lost in quibbling over petty things.

The Buddha teaches us that our life is like a dream. If we want a dream of enjoyment, we are like children blowing colorful bubbles; every bubble is beautiful but lasts only for a short moment. No matter how beautiful the dream may be, we still must face the real world when we awaken. We must deal with reality and use our wisdom to choose the right path. We must avoid both extremes of greedy with endless desires and stingy while unwilling to give.

Many years ago, we helped an old retired school principal who had continued to live in his school's housing facilities even after retirement. The school repeatedly asked him to move, but he would not. Finally, the school offered him a small, shabby old hut on the school premises, thinking he might refuse and leave because of the primitive conditions. Surprisingly, he accepted the arrangement just to save on housing expenses.

The man was in the final stage of liver cancer when Tzu Chi volunteers came into contact with him. There was no one to care for him, so Tzu Chi volunteers checked him into the hospital for treatment. During his hospital stay, the volunteers looked after him and supplemented his meal expenses until he passed away. The hospital asked Tzu Chi to help with his funeral arrangements. So the volunteers cleaned his body and changed his clothing. A hospital staff member produced a shabby-looking package wrapped in old newspapers that the old man had left behind, and asked Tzu Chi volunteers to take care of it too.

The volunteers discovered that the old newspapers and rags held gold and a bank passbook for an account with more than US$5,000. At that time, US$5,000 was a large sum that could purchase several houses. Later, Tzu Chi found out that the man had a son living abroad who had not come back for a long time. Every year the man sent money to his son but he never let his son know how much money he had. He was so thrifty he was reluctant to spend money on himself. In the end, Tzu Chi volunteers gave all his belongings to the township office and contacted his son to come claim it. Unused wealth is as good as trash. It is difficult to understand why he spent his life that way.

Moreover, greed for wealth can also cause harm. There is one such case in a Buddhist sutra. One day the Buddha was walking along a drainage ditch by the roadside and Ananda, the Buddha's cousin and disciple, was following behind him. Suddenly the Buddha turned around and said to Ananda, "A poisonous snake."

Ananda looked into the ditch and replied respectfully, "Indeed it is a poisonous snake."

A father and son walking behind them overheard their conversation. They also looked into the ditch, but discovered it was a jar of gold. They happily took the gold home. Soon afterwards, government officers came to their house to question them, "We heard that there is a jar of gold in your house that was stolen from the national treasury."

The father and son answered anxiously, "No, we did not steal it. We found it in a ditch."

Because they could not prove that they had not stolen the jar, they were arrested and found guilty. The father sighed and said, "It was indeed a poisonous snake."

"Yes, we encountered a poisonous snake," the son concurred.

The officer in charge of the case felt the statement peculiar and asked, "What are you talking about?" The father told him what had happened. After further investigation, the officer decided that they were innocent and released them.

The Buddha used this story to teach practitioners, "A greedy mind is like an invisible poisonous snake. One should eliminate greedy desires to avoid calamities."

We often encounter tangible and intangible calamities because of greed. Therefore, even during an economic depression, we should use this story to teach ourselves to eliminate our greed and return to our original nature. In other words, we should revert back to our pure and clean innate nature, work diligently, and live frugally so that we can live healthily and safely.

Once, a Tzu Chi volunteer was laid off from his job. His family always worked hard and lived frugally. They ate simple meals and never threw away leftovers. They took home tables and chairs that others discarded, fixed them up, and used them. Their children read second-hand books and worked with them at the recycling center. They valued a happy life together over indulging in materialistic desires. Although out of a job, the man was rich in his heart, because he could volunteer during his period of unemployment. He felt happy every day. Is this not a rich life?

If we choose to live simply and peacefully, what else do we need? We should cherish the earth with gratitude and treasure every object with love. To a wise person, there is no such thing as "trash" in the world. He can make good use of everything so that natural resources will always be in abundance. Unfortunately, most people are extremely wasteful. They blindly follow fashion trends and spend lavishly to buy unnecessary merchandise. They do not cherish what they have, and they throw away things that have not yet broken.

Our vanity drives us to chase after the latest fashion trends. We should not buy anything on impulse. Instead, we should buy only what we need. Because they are necessities, we should cherish them and use them with care. Even when these things are old and worn out we can still find creative ways to reuse them.

I know of an elderly lady who cherishes everything. For example, she will cut out the good section of a worn-out bed sheet and make a beautiful cushion by following the original floral pattern. She carefully takes apart broken umbrellas, recycles the metal spokes, and uses the fabric to make raincoats. If she has a damaged handbag, she will cut, mend, and sew it into a new bag. She even sews the edges of her bags with electric wires to make them sturdier and prettier.

This is not only a virtue of cherishing things with her skill, but also a show of her wisdom. Since she was young, her creativity has allowed her to find ingenious ways to fix up used objects. There is no trash in her hands. She saves the hot water she uses to wash her face in the morning in a discarded, but usable, thermos bottle. Then, throughout the day, she has warm water for washing her hands.

Some people complain that they are old and useless, but this elderly lady never thinks that way. She and her husband are both over eighty years old, and have been volunteering together at the recycling center for more than a decade. They are indeed treasures of humanity.

This elderly lady cherishes human relationships and natural resources as well as the objects she uses every day. She employs her wisdom and ability to work, and treats each object she encounters as a beautiful piece of art. Her virtues of cherishing blessings, treasuring objects, and reusing everything are great examples for us to follow. If we can all do this as she does, our natural resources will not be depleted so quickly. Reusing goods will ensure that the materials we need will not run out.

Living in this world, we should learn to overcome our desires and use our wisdom to cherish all objects. Then we will always have plenty of natural resources.

Section 3 - Be a Benefactor to Others

People who have the karmic affinity to know one another should be good friends and benefactors to each other. They should guide each other onto the right path. For example, if you are my good friend, when I do something wrong, you will promptly remind me and correct me. And when you make a mistake, I will also tell you earnestly. Each of us will gratefully and happily accept the other person's criticism. When everyone follows rules, then there will be no deception, fraud, or fighting in our society and people will get along peacefully and harmoniously.

In addition, we should devote ourselves to helping those in need. Everyone has the potential to love other people. As long as we can bring out the unlimited love in each of us, we are able to support and help one another. When we work in unity, I believe nothing is difficult in the world.

● Explore Our Unlimited Potential

Many people use excuses such as health problems or inconvenience to avoid taking action. While they make excuses, time slips away and dreams are lost. Mr. Zhang suffers from poor eyesight, so he can only see a few centimeters in front of him, yet he was determined to become a Tzu Chi volunteer and put his caring heart into action.

At one of Tzu Chi's activities, Mr. Zhang participated in a sign language song performance. It is easy for other people to learn sign language; they can watch the teacher's demonstration as they listen to the music. But it is very difficult for Mr. Zhang since he can hardly see. He became depressed sometimes because of his slow progress, but he was determined to overcome the challenge. After practicing over and over, he finally mastered the signs for the entire song. When he performed on stage, he matched the others' signing perfectly. No one could tell that had weak eyesight, and that he accomplished this by hearing alone.

Mr. Zhang takes on all the regular duties of Tzu Cheng Faith Corps volunteers. Whatever the others do, he can also accomplish the task. When he weeds the garden, he bends over close to the ground to look carefully and make sure he does not mistakenly pull up planted grass. When he is on night duty, he asks other Tzu Chi volunteers to take him around the building complex to familiarize himself with the surroundings, such as the locations of light switches, outlets, windows, and doors. No job is too difficult for him. It is very touching to know how he goes about his work with a loving heart. This is what I mean when I say, "'See with our ears. Be mindful of everything.'"

Ms. Lü lives in southern Taiwan. She is hard of hearing due to tinnitus. She has sought medical help for many years without any improvement. The problem plagued her for quite a while, but eventually she learned to live with it. She now regards the ringing in her ears as music. Ms. Lü is a dedicated Tzu Chi media volunteer. Since she can see clearly, she takes photographs and writes articles to document Tzu Chi's historical moments. As a witness to history, the work she does with her pen, notebook, and camera is very significant.

That is why I often say that everyone has innate ability and potential. However, if we only want to live an easy life and avoid hard work, our ability and potential will gradually go to waste.

There was a seventy-year-old veteran with cancer who had trouble going about his day-to-day life. A former colleague lived next door to him, and would often go care for him. Once, when the area was flooded, the neighbor rushed over and found his bed was about to be covered by water. The neighbor immediately carried him on his back and climbed up to the attic.

After the water had receded, Tzu Chi volunteers went to visit the old veteran. The neighbor who carried him up to the attic asked the Tzu Chi volunteers to help bring him down.

The stairway to the attic was narrow and steep; it was not easy to carry him down, even with the help of several young volunteers. Under the watchful eye and careful guidance of more volunteers downstairs, they finally carried the ailing veteran down.

"How did you take him up to the attic?" the volunteers asked.

The neighbor replied, "I have no idea how I did it. Even looking at the steep stairway now makes my legs shake."

The ailing veteran and his former colleague were about the same age. Actually the ailing veteran was bigger and heavier than his neighbor. In an emergency, the neighbor was so focused on helping and carrying his friend to safety that he never considered his physical ability to do so. Is this not a demonstration of one's innate ability and potential?

This incident shows that as long as we are willing to utilize it, our power to help others as well as ourselves is both real and inexhaustible.

● Confidence in Doing Good Deeds

Love is a smooth, broad boulevard. But if we lack love, life's path is bumpy and difficult.

Some think that it is hard to do good deeds and help others. Even though you want to help others, some people may say, "You are foolish not to spend the money on yourself." After a while, your loving heart and kind thoughts will start to waver because of external influence. You begin to ask yourself why you waste your hard-earned money to help others.

In life, there are things we must do and things we must not do. We should actively do the things that must be done. When we take hold of the moment to make contributions, we will learn a great deal, and we will be happy and at ease. So when we are sure of the direction we have chosen, we should maintain our faith. We should have selfless faith in our family, our society, and our country; we must believe that no matter how tough the situation, it will change some day.

Where there is a will, there is blessing and strength. Great love through teamwork can make a difference, but it requires everyone to take action. Action strengthens our faith. Otherwise, if we talk the talk without walking the walk, we will easily give up our beliefs when we face the temptation of material gains or when we encounter any difficulties.

There is a primary school in San Francisco in which more than ninety percent of the students are from poor immigrant families. These families seriously lack food and supplies. Tzu Chi volunteers started caring for the students with book donations at first, then followed with frequent distributions of food and uniforms.

Ms. Huang often went with Tzu Chi volunteers to visit the school, and one day she brought her daughter along. A girl who was about the same age as her daughter approached them and asked, "Can you please adopt me? I have no food to eat." Ms.

Huang was shocked.

On another occasion, Ms. Huang witnessed a student stealing packets of ketchup, then saw her mix the ketchup with water to drink. She also saw a girl steal a handful of uncooked rice and put it into her mouth. She asked this girl why she did that, and the girl replied that she was hungry. These children were not stealing because they were bad. They were driven to it by starvation.

Ms. Huang felt that she should rearrange her life so that she could devote more time to Tzu Chi and take care of children in need. At that time, she was a senior executive at an international pharmaceutical company. When she presented her letter of resignation, her boss was stunned and tried to convince her to stay.

"Which company is trying to hire you? What salary are they offering? We will give you a raise!"

"None of these," she answered. "My salary is high enough here. I am grateful and satisfied. I just wish to devote myself fully to Tzu Chi."

"What is Tzu Chi?" her boss asked.

Ms. Huang then told him about Tzu Chi's relief efforts, and described the poor living conditions of those who suffer. Her boss still could not understand. He wondered whether doing good deeds really makes a person happy and whether it is more valuable than having a high-paying job.

Nonetheless, Ms. Huang had already made up her mind to resign and become a full-time Tzu Chi volunteer. Since then, she has gone to the school every day with another Tzu Chi volunteer to help provide a better learning environment for the students. Tzu Chi volunteers pass out food backpacks for the students every Friday so that they will have food to eat at home over the weekend. At school, they teach the students Tzu Chi's humanistic culture and help them with their schoolwork. They not only help the students improve their grades, they also emphasize character education by teaching the students to follow rules and regulations, have good manners, cherish the earth, and recycle. That particular elementary school has now become a very good school in its district.

It is commendable that Ms. Huang gave up her personal profits and comforts to devote herself joyfully. Life is short and impermanent. When we see suffering in the world, we should bring forth our love and take action to help the needy. When everyone's strength is combined, we can truly improve our environment. This is the ecology of love.

● **Rich at Heart**

In this world, very few people would consider their lives perfect and free from remorse. Even those with enormous riches and everything going their way cannot avoid regrets connected with birth, aging, illness, and death. Actually, it is better to be rich at heart than to be rich with money. No matter what we face along life's natural course, we must be content and grateful. A life with long-lasting affection and great love in our hearts is the happiest life.

If we constantly worry about losses and gains, then even if we have great wealth we are poor at heart and live in affliction. During global financial crises, the stock market fluctuates up and down. This makes many people worry and suffer. On the other hand, if people go about their business according to their true capabilities, live simple and frugal lives, and help others when they can, they will be content and truly rich.

Mrs. Cai has a daughter who gave birth to a boy and a girl. Her daughter's family should have been happy; unfortunately, her son-in-law was irresponsible and did not take care of the family. Furthermore, Mrs. Cai's granddaughter was born with severe epilepsy caused by a shortage of oxygen in her brain at birth. Dealt with these blows, Mrs. Cai's daughter fell into a depression. Mrs. Cai could not bear to see her daughter suffer, so she took her daughter and her grandchildren home to take care of them. We can only imagine what a heavy burden she had to shoulder.

Mrs. Cai's case was referred to Tzu Chi by a social worker in a Kaohsiung hospital. After receiving Tzu Chi's care and assistance,

Mrs. Cai's daughter recovered from her depression and started to work as a health aide. Her income has greatly reduced Mrs. Cai's financial burden. Though he is still a student, Mrs. Cai's grandson also works to supplement the family income. They all work very hard to make a living.

In order to allow her daughter to concentrate on her work, Mrs. Cai has taken full responsibility to care for her epileptic granddaughter, who is now seventeen years old. When her granddaughter was small, Mrs. Cai was able to hold her or carry her on her back, but it is increasingly hard for Mrs. Cai to do that now. The doctor has said that as the granddaughter gets older, her weight will keep increasing and her organs will gradually deteriorate: her disability will become worse.

Mrs. Cai has never given up caring for her granddaughter, even though it is getting more and more difficult. She says, "Since she had the affinity to be born into our family, we should take good care of her." Not only does Mrs. Cai understand the karmic law of cause and effect, she can accept adverse fate gracefully. She really possesses a big heart and a pure mind. In addition to taking care of her granddaughter, Mrs. Cai uses her time for recycling work, After selling the recyclables, she lets her granddaughter put a few coins into the bamboo piggy bank herself, so that she can also help others. Although they do not have much, Mrs. Cai is able to supplement the family income through her labors, and save a little at a time to help others.

As long as we are healthy in both body and mind, we can be rich even if we have no money. Mrs. Cai is old and her back is hunched, yet she is not scared of hardship. As long as she can still work, she does whatever is needed. From helping herself and receiving help to helping others, she lives such a rich spiritually life. A person is certainly blessed when he or she can face adversity with an understanding heart.

How much do we need for our daily living? There is no standard measure. As long as we have love in our hearts and live simply and frugally, we have the ability to help others. In Yilan, there is an old couple in their eighties. They depend on each other since the husband cannot hear well and the wife cannot see clearly. Their child was born with autism. They cared for him until he died just past the age of forty after taking some over-the-counter medicine for a common cold.

Tzu Chi volunteers have cared for the old couple for more than ten years by helping with housecleaning. Whenever the old couple needs assistance, the volunteers respond quickly. They treat the old couple as their own parents. The couple is kind and friendly. Although their life has been hard, they are able to live happily with love and care from Tzu Chi volunteers.

One day a Tzu Chi volunteer came to visit them. The old woman said to her, "You seem to be very busy."

"Yes, I am on my way to collect donation money," answered

the volunteer.

"What is donation money?" The old woman asked.

The volunteer explained that the money Tzu Chi uses for charity is collected from kind donors: a little here and a little there. The old woman realized that her financial aid came from the efforts of many people who collected donations from people a few dollars at a time. She told the volunteer to stop her financial aid.

She said, "Our cost of living is less than forty dollars a month, and we receive senior citizen subsidies from the government each year, so Tzu Chi does not need to give us aid anymore."

She also pledged to donate fifteen dollars a month. Worried about their livelihood, the volunteer suggested that she donate only three dollars each month. The old woman insisted on donating fifteen dollars. She said, "You come to see us often. If something should happen, why should we worry about not having money?" She is indeed wise and compassionate.

No matter how much money you have, when you are too sick to move, it is useless to be staring at your money. That is why the old couple decided to start helping others while they still could. Later they installed the Da Ai Television channel because the wife wanted to listen to Dharma teachings. Due to her poor eyesight, she sits very close to the television. The husband cannot hear well, but he is in good health. He often goes out to pick up bottles and cans while his wife sorts recyclables at home. Doing recycling work together, they lead a peaceful and worry-free life.

I sincerely wish everyone in this world can be a Bodhisattva and the earth can become a Pure Land of Bodhisattvas. Then, no one will suffer any more. Some may think that it is not easy for these wishes to come true. Actually, if we bring forth our love and influence others to work together and extend a helping hand to those who suffer, everyone can be a benefactor to others.

Chapter 7 - Achieving Harmony among People, Matters, and Principles

In life, we cannot avoid interactions with people. When our minds are narrow, then nothing can get through. But if we can let go, what trouble is there? Planting good seeds enables us to reap good fruits, and forming good affinities allows us to attain good retributions. This is the cycle of cause and effect. In order to create good affinities with others, we should first eliminate the habits of hatred and anger, and begin to practice tolerance.

Tolerance is not an easy thing to practice. Let us look at the word in Chinese. Chinese characters are so clever: the character for "tolerance" (忍) depicts a knife (刀) sticking into a heart (心). Removing the knife from the heart without causing harm would truly require tremendous skill.

Some people are so kind and friendly that when you see them, you just light up. Superintendent Zhang of Yuli Tzu Chi General Hospital is one such person. In addition to running the hospital, he often participates in free clinics and goes on house calls. Yet, no matter how busy he is, he never forgets to smile.

The doctors and nurses of Yuli Tzu Chi General Hospital regularly conduct house calls to serve those living in remote areas. As they do, they often visit a ninety-year-old man who lives alone, even though he is healthy. During one of their visits, they noticed the man's hands and legs were red and swollen, so they suggested that he seek treatment. The man was not happy with the suggestion and replied firmly, "I study Chinese herbal medicine. I will treat it myself."

Upon returning to the hospital, the staff reported this incident to Superintendent Zhang, who immediately rushed to see the old man. Upon seeing him, Superintendent Zhang bowed respectfully and extended friendly greetings. His courtesy and friendliness made the old man take a liking to him, and immediately shortened the distance between them. Superintendent Zhang chatted with the old man and praised his studies in Chinese medicine. Delighted, the old man let Superintendent Zhang examine his swollen hands.

Superintendent Zhang saw that his hands were not only swollen, but had also developed a drug rash. He knew that it must itch, so he took out some rubbing alcohol and wetted a cotton ball. He asked, "Is it itchy? Would it be all right if I dab this cooling liquid on your hands?" The old man consented with pleasure.

The superintendent continued, "Although Chinese herbal medicine is good, the rash is irritating you, and once the skin breaks, an ulcer will follow. How about I put some ointment on the rash first?" Having formed a good impression about the superintendent from the very beginning, the old man agreed to everything the superintendent suggested. Superintendent Zhang deftly treated the swollen area, and a week later it was completely healed.

We must always be big-hearted. Whenever we deal with something, let us not argue or lose our temper. Instead, let us consider it our duty. True tolerance is not "tolerating until you can no longer bear," but rather "tolerating without effort." If we can do this, our interactions with others will be free of obstacles.

I often say, "When we perfect our relationships and actions, then our principles are perfect." When we interact with others and handle our affairs in harmony, then our principles are correct. Such is the pure, well-rounded heart.

Section 1 – Getting Along Under the Same Roof

A Taiwanese adage says, "Parents' love for their children is like a stream of ever-flowing water." Just as water continually flows downstream, parents unconditionally give of themselves to their children and never ask for anything in return. They are frugal and hard on themselves for the sake of their children. They have only one desire, to save more money to pass on to their children and grandchildren. Yet, do children understand their parents' intentions?

Conventional wisdom states, "Wealth does not last beyond three generations." Parents should realize that passing on virtue is better than passing on wealth. In Chinese society, the most admirable virtue is family ethics. Parents love and take good care of their children when they are young. In return, children should repay their parents' grace and be filial when they grow up. A happy family is one in which children are filial to parents and elders, husband and wife live in harmony, and parents raise their children with love and wisdom.

● Parents Are Role Models for Their Children

People used to say, "After giving birth to a child, the mother will tell lies for three years." This describes just how much parents adore their children. For example, when a child is babbling out his first sounds, the mother will think that her child is talking. I once saw filial children behaving in the same manner. No one was sure whether an ailing mother was nodding her head, because it was not obvious to people outside the family. Yet the daughter remarked excitedly, "Yes, mother is nodding her head! She heard us!"

Parents are role models for their children. How they treat their own parents serves as an example to their children. For this reason, parents should seize every opportunity to be filial to their own parents. We should treat parents like living Buddhas in our home, by always paying close attention to their daily needs and looking after them.

I know an orchard owner and his wife who work hard every day to make a living. During the day, their mother helps take care of their children. As soon as the wife comes home, however, she immediately wants the children to come to her side. If her children still stay close to their grandmother, she scolds them for relying on her too much. Sometimes the grandmother would sometimes cook something special for the children. When the wife came home, she would take it away and cook something else. She was often rude to her mother-in-law right in front of the children.

When her husband witnessed such incidents, he felt bad. He told his wife, "You should be kinder to mother."

She replied matter-of-factly, "Our children are like the fruit in our orchard. We work hard in the hopes of bearing fruit. Once we have fruit, we should love and cherish them." Her response made her husband feel helpless.

One day her husband went to the orchard and chopped the roots of a tree. The leaves and fruit gradually withered and fell off. The wife cried out in shock, "What happened? The fruit all fell off the tree!"

"Didn't you see that the roots are severed?" her husband asked.

"Why are the roots severed?"

"Because I chopped them off."

"You idiot, how could you chop off the tree's roots? The fruit all fell off!"

He answered, "You are right. We must take care of the tree's roots just as we must take care of our own roots. My parents brought me into this world, and my mother worked hard to raise me. Filial piety is the foundation of being human. If you cannot be filial, it is as if your roots have been chopped off. How can you bear good fruit?"

The wife thought over what her husband said and admitted that she had been wrong. Since then, she has been a filial daughter-in-law.

Parents must take responsibility for their family and raise their children with love. At the same time, children must be filial to their parents and elders. There is a Tzu Chi couple that lives together with the man's father. The wife is a Tzu Chi commissioner and the husband is a Tzu Cheng Faith Corps member. Every morning, the old father goes out to exercise. When he comes home, the daughter-in-law greets him, "It's cold out, Father. Were you dressed warmly enough? You must be exhausted." She helps him sit down, brings him a towel, and serves him tea.

The father-in-law asks, "Now that you've already finished the household chores, what are your plans for today?" The couple often tell him about Tzu Chi activities, which he enjoys hearing. When his young grandson comes home from school, the child immediately hugs his grandfather, who hugs him back and lovingly asks about his schoolwork. The boy cheerfully tells him, "I earned the highest score on this exam." The boy's father wants to reward him with cash, but the boy says he will save the money in his piggy bank to do good deeds.

This family is harmonious and happy. The daughter-in-law is respectful to her father-in-law, as is the son to his father. They show their care with a gentle voice. The grandfather is happy, the parents are kind, and the child is filial. This is truly a blessed family.

● **Genuine Tolerance Resolves Conflicts**

There is an interesting story about two brothers who wanted to divide up their inheritance. Since their parents had passed away, these two brothers asked their great-uncle's help to ensure an equitable distribution of the family belongings. Neither the brothers nor their wives were willing to yield. Feeling helpless, the great-uncle said, "Let us bring out all the family assets and allocate them one by one." Then he pointed to the items one by one and asked the brothers who should get it. But they continued to bicker over each item, wanting their share in everything. Finally, the great-uncle had had enough. He broke a plate in two and said to the brothers, "Here, this half of the plate is for you, and this half is yours." As he went to break the tables, chairs, and clothing in half, the two brothers decided it was better not to divide their property.

Sibling ties are too close to be divided. We can divide objects, but can our hearts truly be separated? Unfortunately, our minds are always discriminating and calculating, which can damage relationships between family members, and even lead to hate and resentment. If everyone squares off as enemies, how can our world be harmonious?

During the Tang Dynasty, Emperor Gaozong thought highly of filial piety. During his reign, there was a family by the name of Zhang that had nine generations living under the same roof. One day the emperor was out on an inspection trip and stopped by Zhang's house. The emperor asked, "How do you keep such a large family living in harmony?"

Mr. Zhang did not say a word. He just picked up a brush and wrote the word "tolerance" one hundred times. Seeing this, the emperor was moved to tears. Indeed, everyone in a large extended family must tolerate one another in order to achieve harmony. It is of no use if only one person tolerates the others. And harmony cannot be reached if but one member does not practice tolerance. Therefore, everyone must tolerate everyone else. Only with tolerance can we have a broad mind.

In a traditional society, family ethics are highly valued. In modern times, however, people pay less attention to family values and often do as they please. I see many young couples who work hard to get ahead, but once they achieve financial success, they can no longer get along with one another. As a result, they are easily turned to divorce and they lose their happy and harmonious families. This is truly a pity.

Years ago, when I was teaching the Earth Treasury Sutra, a woman in her sixties said to me, "Master, you don't know how bad my husband was." She then told me how she and her husband had changed after listening to my teachings on the sutra. In the past, she could not help but quarrel with her husband, and her husband would beat her. She lifted her shirt to show me her scars, "Master, the scars have deformed me here and also here. How could I not think of committing suicide?"

"How did you change your way of thinking?" I asked.

"Master, you once said that committing suicide adds to your sins and creates bad karma. So I decided to settle my past bad karma."

"How?" I asked. She explained with an example.

One day, her husband had come home late, and she was very upset at first. But then she thought about the sutra teaching she had just heard, and decided to seize the opportunity to practice what she had learned. She therefore refrained from yelling at her husband. Later, when her husband complained about his stomach aching, she asked, "Have you eaten yet? Shall I cook something for you?"

Her husband was skeptical, "Are you genuinely offering or are you faking it?" he asked.

"Please don't be like that. I really mean it. We have been married for so many years, please give me a chance to serve you. I know eating usually makes you feel better when you have a stomachache."

Her husband said, "Then how about cooking some noodles for me?" So she brought a pot of water to a boil, cooked the noodles, mixed in some tea oil, and brought it to her husband. Seeing her husband sound asleep, she woke him up and encouraged him to eat while the noodles were still hot.

Upon seeing the noodles, her husband said unhappily, "I am thirsty. I want noodle soup."

The wife became irritated. She thought to herself that if it was before, she would not care less whether he ate or not. But now she would be tolerant. She told him, "I will make you a broth so that you can eat the noodles with it."

So she cooked the broth and brought it to him. Her husband complained again, "The soup is too oily. I feel like eating rice porridge."

The wife forced herself to control her temper and said, "Alright. I will eat the noodles myself." She went to wash the rice and cook the porridge.

When the porridge was almost done, she asked her husband, "What would you like with the porridge?"

She brought out the porridge and some pickled cucumbers. Her husband stared at her and said, "You are different today. How come you did not lose your temper? Are you feeling alright?"

She said, "From now on, I will not get mad at you."

"Why won't you become angry?"

"Because I am listening to the Master's teachings on the Earth Treasury Sutra. I do not want to form bad affinities with you. Rather, I want to help you reach enlightenment."

Her husband laughed, "You have only been studying Buddhism for three days, yet you think you can help me reach enlightenment?"

She replied, "Not yet; I have to wait until you are moved." Each day she came to listen to my teachings. Later on, her husband started coming with her.

The wife told me, "My husband has started to repent after listening to the sutras."

I asked her husband, "Have you repented?"

He replied, "I still do not fully understand repentance, but I have already realized that I treated my wife terribly."

I asked, "How about now?"

"Now I should cherish her and thank her every day."

I told him, "That is right. You must cherish your wife as you would your child."

I asked the wife, "How do you treat your husband now?"

"I cherish him as well."

I said, "Yes, you should cherish your husband as you would cherish your own child." If we can do that, then our family will be happy and harmonious.

● Harmonious Hearts Make Everything Flourish

We all must abide by rules. For an individual, it is spiritual practice. For a group of people, it is a system. A family also has rules of behavior. When each family member abides by the family ethics, then parents are kind, children are filial, brothers are close, and sisters-in-law are amiable: the family will of course be harmonious. There is an old saying: "A harmonious family is prosperous." To have a harmonious family, everyone in the family must have their hearts in harmony. In other words, "Harmonious hearts make everything flourish."

As soon as people lose that harmonious relationship, nothing can be accomplished. I often illustrate this point with the following story. A couple owned a bakery and led a very busy life. They often lost their tempers with each other over the smallest incidents. Their daily quarrels and physical fights disturbed the whole neighborhood, so the neighbors asked their mayor to help resolve the problem. The mayor said, "I know we have to solve this problem. But this couple is so rude that the more I ask them to stop, the more fiercely they fight. It is very troublesome."

One day, while the mayor was taking a walk, he saw from afar that the couple was fighting again in their bakery. He overheard the husband shouting angrily, "If you don't do as you're told, I'll take this knife and kill you!"

The wife shouted back loudly, "Go ahead and kill me! I have no desire to live anyway."

The mayor rushed to make peace, but the couple did not listen. Instead, they fought even harder. The mayor suddenly came up with an idea. He shouted to the street, "Fellow villagers, come quickly! Help yourselves to free pastries. Take as many as you like!"

As soon as the couple heard the mayor calling everyone to come take free pastries, they hurriedly asked why he would do such a thing. The mayor replied, "One of you wants to kill the other, and the other wants to die. What good will these pastries be when one of you is dead and the other in jail?"

After hearing the mayor's words, the couple was silent. The mayor continued, "Couples should not fight over trivial matters. You are married because of your karmic affinity, so you should respect each other and resolve your differences with hearts of gratitude. You could not bear to see people come and take your pastries, which shows that you care deeply for the fruits of your labors. As such, you should not throw them away so casually." The couple carefully thought this over and found that the mayor's words made sense. They promised that they would get along with each other and not fight again.

For a family to coexist harmoniously, each member must do his duty and uphold his obligations. When all members clearly understand their duties and mindfully carry out their responsibilities, they can feel calm even after a long and busy day. On the other hand, when one person complains about working too much or thinks his workload is unfair, then he is unable to balance his emotions. As a result, he will have countless afflictions and cause many disputes in the family.

There is an old saying: "Blessings come to a family that is full of goodness." Goodness and love are truly the best family heirlooms. Sunshine on Grass Mountain, a Da Ai Television drama series, depicts the true story of Mr. Gao and his harmonious family. Even though Mr. Gao's father had passed away, he and his brothers continued on as one united family. His oldest brother tried a few times to divide the family assets in hopes of letting each of his younger brothers become independent, but his siblings were unwilling to go their separate ways, because the brothers and their wives all got along so well with one another.

Mr. Gao is in the construction business. Once, one of his friends defaulted on a loan of several million dollars. None of his family members blamed him for the tremendous loss. Instead, they assumed the loss together. They helped and supported one another to overcome this hardship. Mr. Gao's business eventually recovered because he had a united family to support him, and siblings who took care of one another.

The Buddha said that life is suffering. Those who are truly understanding and tolerant will be able to get along with others. A harmonious life is truly a blessing.

 ## Section 2 – Networking on Campus

Our future relies on education, and our society relies on capable people, who are nurtured through education. Nurturing children is like growing trees. Seeds require soil, water, sunshine, air, and care in order to sprout and grow into big, healthy trees.

Education requires a positive environment, so that everything that children see and hear in their daily lives sets a positive example for them. At home, parents provide the mold. At school, teachers provide the model. When children have good examples to learn from and emulate, they can cultivate ideal values.

Everyone has the ability to love. Whether at home or in school, we should let children learn how to love and respect themselves and others. If children only receive love, then over time they will take it for granted. They will lack the ability to love and respect themselves, let alone love and respect others. Therefore, in addition to passing on academic knowledge, teachers need to teach principles of benevolence, integrity, manners, ethics, and morals. Only when parents, teachers, and society promote these same principles together with one heart will they be effective.

● Parents, Teachers, and Students Join Efforts

When teaching thrives and morals flourish, the world has hope. Therefore, education must focus on *teaching with propriety and guiding with principles*. It is said that etiquette constitutes the real truth. We should first teach children manners and etiquette so that they can know and understand truth.

Teaching etiquette requires a joint effort from parents, teachers, and students. In the past, parents always urged their children to listen attentively to their teachers. They reminded their children to keep their teachers' instructions in mind and apply them in their daily lives. When children are reminded every day by their parents to respect their teachers, they will naturally respect them.

In school, teachers set an example with their own conduct. When teachers meet, they greet each other and exchange bows to set a good example for their students. Seeing this, students will understand etiquette, and bow too when they see their teachers. This is the proper etiquette for greeting on campus. In addition, teachers teach etiquette and ethics in the classroom. Students see the examples their teachers set for them and hear about good deeds from exemplary people. Immersed in an environment where people uphold their duties and do good deeds, students can learn truth through practicing etiquette.

Why are there so many problems with youth today? It is not because children cannot be taught, nor is it because every child is mischievous. In fact, each of us is responsible. If teachers lack a sense of mission in their instruction, then they begin to feel that the more they teach, the more troubles they encounter. When teachers slack off in their teaching, they stop disciplining students. In other cases, parents spoil their children so much that they go to school to complain when their children are shown even a little discipline. This can turn into a vicious cycle. On the other hand, when teachers do their best and take responsibility for instructing students, and the parents respect the teachers, then not only can children receive an education of love, this loving feeling can influence families. Such is the cycle of love.

Over the years, the Tzu Chi Teachers Association has encountered many instances where a student's parents' marriage was in crisis or a student's family was on the verge of splitting apart. Due to some teacher's passion for teaching and genuine caring for his students, the teacher took the initiative to understand the student's problems at home. Through counseling for the parents, these teachers were often able to make their students' families whole again. I always like to share Mr. You's story as an example. Mr. You, who lives in Pingtung, was a very strict teacher who often doled out corporal punishment to his students. After joining Tzu Chi, he learned about Jing Si Aphorisms and started to apply them to his life. After thoroughly digesting the aphorisms, he taught them to his students. He stopped corporal punishment altogether, and has seen some unexpected results.

Mr. You's class is full of students that the school had given up on, but under Mr. You's loving and patient guidance, the students have gradually changed themselves.

The parents of one of Mr. You's students were constantly fighting. After one particularly bad fight, they considered divorce. The student took this opportunity to practice what he had learned from his teacher. He wrote two notes. He posted one on his father's closet door and the other on his mother's mirror. In the morning, his father saw a note on his closet door: Anger is momentary insanity. His mother found a note on the mirror: Do not punish yourself with the mistakes of others. The parents showed each other the notes, and smiled to each other when they read them.

They realized that parents' fighting sets a bad example for the children, so they agreed to avoid quarreling from then on. Later, at a Back-to-School Night, as other parents shared their experiences, they discovered that many families had similar stories.

Parents should apply the wisdom of Bodhisattvas in treating their children, and they should accept other children as if they were their own. They should not worry only about their own children, nor should they reject other children. They should give love appropriately with an open and selfless heart.

No one can survive without water. Love should be like clear water, but, like water, it cannot be in excess. For example, some parents want their children to focus only on studying, so they over-protect their children and do not let them do any household chores. As a result, their children do not even know how to wash their own clothes. How can these children experience the true meaning of love? Excess love can turn into a burden and weigh down the children. Or, they may get used to it and take it for granted. We should give love appropriately and properly guide our children to become well-educated, polite, and full of self-respect.

There is a student named Wu who lives in the remote mountains of Taitung County. Her family is poor, and after her mother passed away, her father took on odd jobs in the mountains to stay close to his children. Wu helps out with the household chores and takes care of her younger siblings after school.

Having earned the highest score in the whole county on the Basic Competence Test for Junior High School Students, Wu qualified to attend the very prestigious Taipei First Girls' High School in Taipei. However, she chose instead to attend a local high school in Taitung due to her family's financial situation. After her story was reported on the news, Tzu Chi volunteers immediately visited her family to gain a better understanding of her situation.

Her father works hard to take good care of his family, and his three children are all smart and considerate. Although their home is poor, it is warm. Wu loves her father and is very grateful to her teacher. She always says that she has two fathers: one is her teacher, who frequently tutors her in math after school and constantly encourages her. Her teacher educates her with the love of a parent, nurturing and guiding her. Self-respecting children like Wu are the future talents and hope of our society.

● A Report Card of Love

In the teaching profession, educators should uphold the spirit of expounding wisdom, and guide students to tread the correct path. In life, we must walk the right path so that our lives can be broadened. If we go astray, we will hurt ourselves and harm society as well.

The purpose of teaching is to open up the ignorant mind. We all begin as ignorant children and learn whatever we are taught. For this reason, we must inspire our children to be kind, and carefully nurture them as they grow.

Many teachers and students take advantage of summer and winter vacations to travel abroad for studying or sightseeing. But how does this help or inspire them? It may broaden their perspective, but does it allow their mind to see a genuine picture of the world?

Tzu Chi once organized an educational trip to Danzhai County in Guizhou, China. Tzu Chi has cultivated a good affinity with this county for many years. Not only did we help build schools there, but we also regularly provide need-based scholarships to primary and secondary school students. Therefore, our bonds with this community are strong. One year, the Tzu Chi Teachers Association organized a group to visit Guizhou during summer vacation. The group consisted of seventy or eighty teachers and students from Tzu Chi University, Tzu Chi High School, and Tzu Chi College of Technology.

Before they left, I told the teachers, "This trip is a rare opportunity. Help the students understand how other children live and study."

In Danzhai, some students lived in the school dormitories because their homes were far away. The dormitories were old and shabby with leaky roofs. There were no mattresses on the bunk bed frames, so students had to bring their own wooden boards to sleep on. Even when attending class, students had to bring their own chairs. Moreover, the boarding students cooked their own meals. They went home once a week, and brought rice and vegetables to school when they came back. Two or three students would form a group to cook and eat together. They cooked simple dishes by putting everything in a big pot over a small stove.

The students witnessed the local children washing their own clothes in a small basin of water, scrubbing away at the soiled areas. Tzu Chi teachers asked, "Why do you use so little water to wash?" A student explained, "Saving water saves money for the school." These students were content with what they had and realized their own blessings. They had few desires, even as they lived and studied in a difficult environment. They understood that they had to study hard in order to overcome poverty and hardship.

Upon returning from the trip, our students shared their experiences. They said that they had seen the most innocent smiles. They had witnessed how the Guizhou students ate their rice without wasting a single grain, even using the last vegetable in the bowl to scrape and clean out the bowl. They never complained about how simple their meals were. Instead, they were grateful to their parents and appreciative of their hard work. This gratitude demonstrated that their hearts were unpolluted; that is why their smiles were so innocent.

The Tzu Chi students learned that the scholarships we gave to the primary school students was about twenty-four dollars per year. One student commented, "I am ashamed. My glasses cost more than one hundred dollars, my T-shirt was more than thirty dollars, my blue jeans cost more than one hundred dollars, and this pair of brand-name sneakers was also a couple hundred dollars. The total value of what I am wearing now could provide scholarships to fifteen students for a whole year." From then on, the students who had gone on the trip started to live frugally. Through witnessing the hardships of others, they learned to cherish their blessings and feel grateful for what they have.

With so many people in the world, some worry that it will take too long to inspire everyone to love others. We should remember that a big tree grows from a tiny seed, so everyone can spread the seeds of love.

In 1998, the Dominican Republic was devastated by Hurricane Georges. Tzu Chi USA quickly sent an aid team and has continued to offer support to this day. Unable to bear seeing local children deprived of an education and foraging for food on the garbage mountain every day, our volunteers decided to help build schools and improve the environment. Over the years, this place has become neat, beautiful, and full of energy.

Tzu Chi volunteers often visit Dominican Republic to care for the locals. Not only have they seen the students progress from primary to secondary school, they have also provided food, uniforms, book bags, and school supplies from time to time. The principal and teachers have been deeply moved by the Tzu Chi volunteers. The school has always maintained a lively atmosphere.

The locals cherish their opportunity for education, so they highly value the graduation ceremony. At the ceremony, each graduate dons cap and gown, and demonstrates the results of etiquette education by respectfully serving tea to teachers, parents, and Tzu Chi volunteers who travel from the United States to attend the ceremony.

When Typhoon Morakot devastated Taiwan in 2009, the children also raised funds to help the typhoon survivors. Seeing volunteers with donation boxes, schoolchildren lined up one after another to donate. These students do not have much, so each one could only donate a few cents. There was one student, however, who donated more than one dollar, so he was asked why he donated so much.

"I heard that the floods in Taiwan caused many schools to collapse and left many people homeless, so we must do our best to help," he replied.

Even though the locals are relatively poor and need help from Tzu Chi, these children's kind thoughts and benevolent acts demonstrate the cycle of love that has formed.

● Fish Twine and Incense Wrapper

There is a story in the Buddhist sutras. One day, the Buddha and his monastic assembly were walking down the road. The Buddha saw a piece of twine in the road and asked the Venerable Ananda to pick it up. As he picked it up, he immediately smelled the stench of rotten fish.

"Ananda, what do you feel?" the Buddha asked.

"This twine is filthy and putrid. It smells like rotten fish," answered the Venerable Ananda.

"Did the rest of you smell it?"

"Yes, we did."

"Why does this twine smell of rotten fish?" the Buddha asked.

Everyone knew that this twine smelled bad because it had been used to tie up fish. The Buddha continued, "Originally this piece of twine did not have such a foul smell, but it was contaminated by the fish it held."

They proceeded on their walk and saw a rolled-up piece of thick paper. The Buddha asked the Venerable Ananda to pick it up. As he opened it, a pleasant smell came forth.

"What do you feel?" the Buddha asked.

"I like it very much. It is fragrant."

"Have you smelled it?" the Buddha asked the others.

"Yes, we smell the sweet aroma."

"Do you know why this piece of paper is so fragrant? Did it have this fragrance to begin with?" They speculated that the piece of paper had been used to wrap sandalwood incense.

This story reminds us that environment is very important. Human nature is pure, yet it becomes defiled as we are tempted by the surrounding environment, which leads to changes in our habits. However, if we can be influenced and moved by a positive environment, then we will be receptive to correct concepts.

I once saw a mother and her daughter on stage sharing their personal experiences. This was a working mother who had high expectations for her daughter, so she disciplined her very strictly. When her teenage daughter went on stage to tell her story, she confessed that she used to resent her mother for nagging her. She did not understand her mother's good intentions, so she caused trouble in school and skipped classes. She gradually made friends with the wrong people and started smoking, drinking, gambling, and even fighting. Her teachers often called home to report her inappropriate behavior, so her mother was quite distraught.

Later, a group of senior Tzu Chi volunteers came to the aid of the distressed mother. They were willing to work with and counsel her young daughter. In the beginning, the daughter resisted them, feeling that they were pretentious. After several months, the daughter realized that the volunteers' love and caring were genuine. Slowly she understood that she was not alone; she was very much loved.

Inspired by the group's love and benevolence, she began to reflect on her own behavior and realized that she should separate herself from her old group of friends. When they came to see her one day, she bravely told them, "Please do not come to see me anymore. This kind of lifestyle is wrong. I need to start my life over. It would be best if we all split up and each started a new life." But they did not listen to her. Instead, they beat her up. Even though she was bloodied and bruised, she did not even fight back.

As she recovered at home, she calmly thought back on the incident. The more she thought, the more she realized that it was worth it to take one beating to gain back a peaceful life. While she was healing, the Tzu Chi volunteers all came to visit her. Their warm embraces and counseling made her realize that she should first apologize to her mother for all of her wrongdoings. Next, she needed to give up her bad habits and study harder. After school each day, she began going with her mother to do recycling work. Now, when people see her delicate face, they cannot imagine the wayward person that she used to be.

An old adage states, "He who stands next to ink will turn

black." Becoming friends with good people leads us to be good. On the other hand, if we stay close to bad people, then we are easily led down the wrong path.

● Be a True Good Friend

I once saw a news report about a group of young people at a karaoke parlor, singing and drinking all night until they eventually became drunk. Someone from the next room gave them a look, and the two parties started fighting. One person was killed and two others were injured. The police rushed to the scene and took both groups in for questioning; young people filled the entire police station. I thought about the parents of all these kids. How worried they must have been, having children staying out all night engaging in unwholesome activities.

All parents want their children to do well and become successful. They hope their children will be smart and well-behaved and will tread the right path, so they can pass through the rebellious teenage years. Actually, there was no such thing as "rebellious years" in the old days. When children saw their parents work hard, they knew that they too should carry out their own responsibilities.

We are very fortunate to have many mature and diligent young people in today's society. I often hear people say, "When I see Tzu

Chi Collegiate Association members, I know that there is hope for our future." These collegiate volunteers are always composed and well-behaved. They are polite, refined, elegant, and graceful. These young people with correct principles should do their best to influence their peers. Because they are of a similar age, they share a common language and can empathize with one another. According to the Dharma, we should all mindfully enlighten those who work with us.

"Enlightening others through cooperative deeds" is one of the Four All-Embracing Virtues, namely charitable offerings, beneficial conduct, loving words, and cooperative deeds. The first, charitable offerings, is not limited only to giving money, but also giving the Dharma and giving courage to free others from fear.

Let us take two female students at Tzu Chi University as an example. During their nursing class, these students volunteered to act as patients so that their teacher could demonstrate how to insert a nasogastric tube. They later explained that this act not only allowed them to experience first-hand what patients feel when receiving a nasogastric tube, but also helped their classmates learn the insertion method.

This act was a charitable offering, even though it was not expressed in cash. It was, rather, a rare display of the giving of Dharma that allowed their classmates to learn how to insert the nasogastric tube. It was also a display of giving courage: When the tube was inserted, the girls felt like vomiting. It was very uncomfortable, but they smiled and told their classmates not to worry. They wanted to create a calm environment for their classmates to continue their learning.

The second virtue is beneficial conduct. We should always consider others first, and help others with empathy. These two students personally experienced the insertion of nasogastric tube, and learned how to do it themselves to reduce the stress of their patients. At the same time, they helped teach the technique to the other students. Their actions were a clear example of beneficial conduct.

The third virtue is loving words. This means that we must use positive words to comfort and counsel others. Most importantly, we must be considerate of others. When speaking kind words, we need a common language to communicate with each other.

The fourth virtue is enlightening others through cooperative deeds. A harmonious world requires everyone striving together. We should not only cultivate ourselves, but also benefit others. We should extend a helping hand to those around us when they encounter difficulties in their work. This is how we enlighten others through cooperative deeds. A genuine cooperative deed is when we help others fulfill their goals.

A student returned to her hometown in Yuli after graduation to serve the locals at Tzu Chi General Hospital. In the beginning, the rigid training led by the senior nurses made her very nervous, and sometimes she could not help but cry. Her classmates would comfort her, saying, "We all love and care about you. We hope that you will mature quickly so that you can take good care of patients." They reassured her often, so she was able to face the training program with courage. This too is a cooperative deed.

Young people are the hope for the future. Each young person should strive to become a good seed and vow to enlighten his friends. That is what a true good friend would do.

Section 3 - Spiritual Practice at the Workplace

Some people live to work, while others work to live. If we work to earn a livelihood, our jobs may not be ideal. When we are not happy at our jobs, our lives will be miserable.

Life is meaningful when we live to work. If we live without a sense of purpose or if we cannot devote ourselves to a field that is needed by society, then we will have lived in vain. Therefore, we should set a goal for our life; we should have a mission. When our workplace is also a place of spiritual practice, our career becomes our place of cultivation. With this mindset, we will learn from our work. This is *learning through doing, enlightenment through learning.*

I worry when people think that they already know everything.

We must not be arrogant. We need to set aside our own ego and work in concert with others. In other words, we should not insist that others follow our lead. If we contradict other's opinions and always think that we are right and others are wrong, we will have tremendous difficulties in carrying out our work.

● Managing by Walking Around

Many years ago, I knew a company chairman who was generous and willing to give, but very stringent with his employees. He thought that he should maintain his authority as a leader so that he could better manage his business and employees. He even grew a beard to make himself look austere.

One Chinese New Year, he came to the Jing Si Abode to help pack relief materials. While everyone was busy packing, I saw a group of Tzu Chi members walk toward us. As they approached, they suddenly froze and dared not step closer. I was puzzled, and signaled for them to come in. At that moment, one of the nuns from the Jing Si Abode took them to the back of the room.

After a while, that nun came in and whispered to me, "Those people are the employees of the chairman. They said that seeing the chairman here makes them afraid."

"Why are they afraid? A chairman and his employees doing volunteer work together: isn't that a good thing?"

The nun replied, "They are afraid that he may think they are here for fun."

After we finished packing, we all sat down for a break. The chairman happened to sit next to me, so I took the opportunity to advise him. "The most successful people do not use their authority and prestige to overpower others. Rather, they win people's hearts and touch them with gentle love."

Upon hearing this, he anxiously asked, "Master, did I do something wrong?"

I replied, "It is not that you did anything wrong. I simply feel that you are too strict, and that your employees are afraid of you."

"No, I love my employees," he said.

I replied, "But you are lacking something."

"What is that?"

"You lack amiability, a smile, and genuine care."

He asked, "If I was like that, how could I manage my employees?"

I said, "Employees should not be managed. They should be loved."

I continued, "A chairman should treat his employees with gratitude. Think about it. If you did not have a cleaning lady to clean the office, then however grand it may be, your office would be a garbage dump. Moreover, your employees all work hard in order to make money for you."

He concurred. "That is true. I should be grateful to my employees." He did as he said. After returning to the office, he started to smile and gradually changed from a stern chairman to a smiling one. He personally led his employees to express gratitude to one another.

During the economic downturn, quite a few companies went bankrupt. He said to me, "I am truly grateful. Now that the economy is bad, many employees in other companies complain about their pay, yet none of my employees have complained." He also said that when he wanted his employees to work overtime for rush orders in the past, no one was willing. They said that they could not care less about the overtime pay. Now he had learned to be considerate. He would say to them, "You have worked hard. Take a break."

Now his employees say to him, "Don't worry, Mr. Chairman. Go ahead and take as many orders as you can. If no one wants to do the work, then we will. We are willing to work overtime, even until midnight, as long as your business flourishes."

"Why?" he asked.

They told him, "Because you are very good to us, and you

often donate to charity. If we work hard, it is as if we are making contributions as well."

In addition to leading people with love and gratitude, I have been promoting the concept of "managing by walking around" for a long time. If someone encounters difficulties, then the manager should walk over to help. It is very important to manage by walking around.

There is an adage: "A lonely bird needs to join with a group." When you come to a new environment, how do you present yourself? The only way is to let go of your ego and be humble. This is especially important for those in positions of power. No matter how outstanding your abilities may be, if you feel that nobody tells you anything or that you are not allowed to do anything, you are placing obstacles on yourself. You must be proactive in asking for help. You must smile sincerely. In this way, you will be easily accepted.

Actually, "a lonely bird needs to join a group" and "getting along well with others" are like two sides of the same coin. If you take the initiative to get along well with a group of people, then you will naturally blend in. On the other hand, if you always isolate yourself and do not get along with the group, you will not win people's hearts and will inevitably be rejected.

Superintendent Zhao Youcheng of Xindian Tzu Chi General Hospital is an excellent example. He recently joined the Tzu Chi medical team, and has literally managed by walking around. He took the initiative to visit each unit of the hospital and showed interest in the employees' work. He asked whether they had any problems or needed any help. In less than ten days, he had gained a good understanding of the hospital's operations. He made everyone in the hospital feel important. One department head commented that no matter where you work, the work is always hard and the environment is about the same. However, if your supervisor is sincere and caring, you will feel happy and warm, and will work contentedly.

If a leader often walks around to care for his employees and help resolve problems, then no matter how big a problem is, it can be resolved.

● Turn Hard Work into Blessings

Sometimes we see people fuss over trivial things and speak matter-of-factly, "Why should I give in to you when you don't give in to me?" Then both sides argue endlessly to get the upper hand. How painful it is!

There was a young lady who was upset with her job. She felt wronged and complained to me in tears. "I work really hard. I do what others are unwilling to do. No matter how tired I get, I can tolerate everything. Yet, even with all my hard work, I have never been complimented. Instead I am criticized for not doing things well. I cannot take this anymore!"

She was crying uncontrollably. I explained to her the art of tolerance. I said, "You are now merely 'tolerating'; you have not reached the stage of 'swallowing'. Not only must you swallow, you have to 'digest' that which bothers you. Only then will you acquire true tolerance."

Ordinary tolerance is like pressing a seed under a rock. The seed is still there; it just cannot sprout and grow for the time being. Therefore, not only must we tolerate, we have to swallow and digest in order to eliminate our resentment. If we hear someone unintentionally say something offensive, yet we intentionally take it to heart, then we are not understanding enough to digest it. As a result, the words will stay in our hearts and continue to hurt us.

Hearing this, her eyes, still filled with tears, began to light up. She said, "I understand now. Because of my inflated ego, I cannot take criticism. I always feel that my colleagues have wronged me, so I get upset easily."

Our egos often get us into trouble. When we do well, we expect to be praised. When we do not do well, we feel inferior. Sometimes we even turn our feelings of inferiority into arrogance. Therefore, regardless of the situation, we must always reflect on whether our ego is overinflated. We should do our work to the best of our abilities. If we have given our best to complete the job, then we can feel peaceful and at ease. Even if the results are not as we expected, we will not become upset.

There is a volunteer who started coming to Jing Si Abode after he retired because his wife was a Tzu Chi commissioner. He has worked happily at the Abode, rain or shine, for many years. He said that volunteering with Tzu Chi is his life's path. Even though he performs simple duties, such as transcription, he has never felt bored. He feels blessed no matter how hard he works.

One day, during the initial stage of building the Dalin Tzu Chi General Hospital, I was walking around the construction site at midday and saw a volunteer moving formwork. I greeted him and said, "It's noon and you are still working. You have worked hard."

The volunteer was very friendly. He put his palms together and said to me, "Master, please do not say to us 'you have worked hard.' Instead, please say 'you are blessed.'"

I asked, "Why say 'you are blessed?' You really have worked very hard."

"Because other volunteers say it that way," he said.

I went along with him and said, "Alright, you are blessed," even though I did not understand the reason behind it at the moment.

Tzu Chi volunteers told me about this story later. One elder who donated his land for the hospital vowed to serve herbal tea to all the workers at the construction site. Every day at three o'clock in the morning he would prepare herbal tea. On hot days, he would use ice to keep the tea cold. On cold days, he would make hot tea. Tzu Chi volunteers would help pour the tea into bottles. As the construction workers arrived for work, they were given the bottles of herbal tea to quench their thirst while they worked.

At the end of the day, Tzu Chi volunteers would stand at the gate and bow to the workers with gratitude, saying, "You have worked hard today."

One day a worker replied candidly, "Indeed we have worked hard. We are working ourselves to death."

One volunteer responded quickly and asked, "Do you know what is being built here?"

The worker answered, "A hospital."

The volunteer asked again, "What is the purpose of this hospital?"

"To save lives."

The volunteer continued, "Yes, saving lives creates blessings. Actually, you are blessed because the construction of this hospital has garnered the love and blessings of Tzu Chi volunteers around the globe. Since you are contributing to the construction, you are participating in the work of saving lives. This is your blessing."

The worker said, "That makes sense. If this is the case, don't say to us, 'you have worked hard.' Instead, you should say, 'you are blessed.'"

The volunteer said, "That is right. From now on, whenever we see you, we will wish you blessings and good health."

The worker was pleased. He said, "When you say 'you are blessed,' I will reply 'I am content.'"

Since that time, these words of blessing have passed down. That is why Tzu Chi volunteers say 'you are blessed' instead of 'you have worked hard.' It is like I always say, *Being able to work is a blessing.*

● **Do Altruistic Work with One Heart**

At Tzu Chi, I come into contact with many people: some are supervisors and some are employees. Hearing their stories, I sense that everyone has his or her problems. Those in the managerial level have their problems and so do those being managed. Actually, everybody needs a common goal. If there is a common goal, and everyone *can work willingly and accept the results joyfully*, then there will be a cycle of goodness.

I often say, "A single person cannot eat all the rice in the world. Likewise, a single person cannot do all the work in the world."

We all hope that our society can become harmonious and our earth can be healthy again, yet this feat cannot be achieved by a single person. Therefore, when we do good deeds we must be grateful to those who share the common goal with us. Without them and their collective strength, how can we accomplish so many things?

Tzu Chi has a "Four Magic Soup." The four ingredients are contentment, gratitude, understanding, and accommodation. We all have our own temperaments and habitual tendencies. We must first transform our own minds and broaden our own hearts. Only then can we really take the Dharma to heart.

We will be grateful once we are content with everything and everyone. A grateful person can easily give selfless love to others. Because he has love in his heart, he can be understanding and accommodate other people's mistakes. For example, Tzu Chi volunteers are occasionally criticized at fundraising events. But they are able to calmly respond, "Thank you, we are grateful." We back down first and then explain to the criticizers after they have calmed down. By doing so, we avoid further dispute or damage.

The Buddhist sutras say that we must enlighten all sentient beings with great love and without discrimination. But accomplishing this work requires certain tools. Of the tools needed, language is the most important. Language allows us to communicate so that we can build relationships with others. Although the varied languages in the world have made communication difficult, we do have a common language: a sincere smile. A sincere smile shows a feeling of closeness. When we add a caring hug, then great love will be free from communication barriers.

Section 4 – Quality Interactions in the Community

In recent years, morals and ethics in our society have been weakening, and environmental problems are worsening. For this reason, we have initiated the "Return to Good Morals" movement to encourage people to be disciplined and courteous. Beginning with ourselves, we must constrain our greed, anger, and delusion, and then extend our love to other people. Genuine love is indispensable in interpersonal relationships.

When I see Tzu Chi volunteers caring for the elderly and the children in their community, I feel that that community is warm and friendly. A friendly community requires everyone to be passionate and caring. Passion is the source of love that allows us to keep giving and caring for others. If we are cold as ice toward one another, our innate love for others will be hindered. But if everyone can be more passionate, our collective kindness and virtue will make the entire community warm and friendly.

● A Land with Blessed People Will Be Blessed

The Buddha teaches us that all beings share collective karma. Karma is what we create. Some people care about society and do good deeds to benefit humankind. They are able to "take from society and give back to society," and create good karma. On the other hand, some people do not tread the right path. They make trouble and commit wrongdoings. They are creating bad karma.

Taiwan is a land of blessings because it has many blessed people. Who are the blessed people? It is those who create blessings by loving others and doing good deeds. Many people wish to become blessed. However, if they have never planted the seeds of blessing, how can they reap its fruit? If we love and cherish Taiwan, we should constantly bless this land and spread the seeds of blessing all over, so that Taiwan can truly become a field of blessings.

Some people are unwilling to create blessings by benefiting others. They think, "It's good enough if my own family is taken care of. I don't need to worry about others." This is the mentality of a selfish person. Think about it. If someone goes astray and does something evil that harms the community, will you be safe? If your neighbors encounter horrible accidents, how can you be sure that your family will not be affected? So you are safe only when all the people in your community are safe.

In many impoverished countries, when natural or man-made disasters strike, even those who are not affected are busy saving themselves. How can they take care of the victims? If people are unable to plant the seeds of blessing, it is difficult to change their circumstances. This is a great pity. Taiwan, on the other hand, is prosperous and has many compassionate people. Although Taiwan is not immune to natural disasters, when one area is hit, people from all over come to help. Everyone lends a hand in a timely manner so that victims can pass safely through the crisis. It is indeed a blessing when a natural disaster does not cause hardships. When everyone does good deeds and creates blessings that benefit others, the weather will naturally be favorable. This is why we say Taiwan is a blessed place.

A proverb tells us that "Those who live in a blessed land will be blessed." But I think it should be "A land with blessed people will be blessed." In other words, no matter how poor and barren the land is, hard-working farmers can fertilize and irrigate the land to enhance the soil and reap a bountiful harvest. On the other hand, if farmers are sluggish in planting their crops, then no matter how rich the soil is, the land will grow nothing but weeds.

Therefore, if each person loves one another and works together in unity, then society will be peaceful, harmonious, and most importantly, rich in love. It is wonderful that Taiwan has so many compassionate people, who can even spread their love to other countries.

In May 2008, Myanmar was severely struck by a tropical cyclone that resulted in many casualties. Large areas of farmland were damaged by the intrusion of seawater. Crops were lost and fields were salinized. The farmers were overwhelmed and helpless. Luckily, continuous rain over the next few days diluted the salt content in the soil. Tzu Chi volunteers eagerly sought and purchased seeds that could resist salt, and distributed them to the farmers in time for planting. Tzu Chi volunteers also distributed fertilizer to the famers four times during the growing season. The farmers accepted the assistance joyfully and worked hard in their fields. Six months later, they not only reaped a bountiful harvest, the yield was twenty percent greater than in previous years.

The farmers harvested the crop with great joy. A farmer plucked six stalks of rice and asked a Tzu Chi volunteer, "Please deliver these personally to Master. We are very grateful for her help."

When I received the rice stalks, I was also pleased with the plump grains. I was even more pleased to know that love had been inspired in the farmers' hearts. Every day many locals donated their loose change. The donations, though minuscule, represented their sincere love. Some people saved up rice to give to others. Before cooking a meal, they would grab a handful of rice and drop it into an earthen jar. They said that their family members still were full even without that one handful of rice; but that saved rice could help poorer villagers who had nothing to eat.

Seeing the villagers in Myanmar contribute with sincerity and love, I saw hope for their country. The more kind-hearted people there are in the region, the more harmonious and prosperous the land will be. That is why we say, "A land with blessed people will be blessed."

● True Personal Warmth

In my early days of charity work, I visited each care recipient personally. When I came to a village, I would ask the locals if they knew so-and-so. No matter whom I asked, once they heard the name they immediately knew who the person was. They would address the person as "uncle so-and-so" or "grandpa so-and-so." I could feel a close relationship and personal warmth among the villagers.

After we told them the purpose of our visit, the villagers would volunteer details about the person's misfortunes and current living conditions. They knew their neighbors very well. In today's society, neighbors are often like strangers, cold and detached. Sometimes they even argue over small matters. Under these circumstances, how can we live a happy and carefree life? If we could go back to the traditional way of living, with the warmth of human touch, then the whole world would be like one big family. How heart-warming it would be!

There is an old general store in the Taiping mountains of Taichung County. Usually a store needs its name to be known. The more well-known a store, the more reputable it is. This store's owners, however, did not seek to make a name for their store, yet the store was immensely popular. The owners are an old couple. The wife is in her seventies, and the husband is over ninety. They sell any goods that are needed by the customers. Their products are inexpensive yet practical and of good quality. What is more, the owners are happy to serve the community. More people come to ask for help than to shop.

Since the mountain roads are difficult to travel and the villagers live far apart, this store has become a drop-off place for the postman and the residents. Villagers often come to the store to pick up their newspapers or check for mail.

In addition to these services, the storeowners are enthusiastic about helping people. Sometimes their neighbors borrow what they need instead of purchasing it. The wife even lends them brand-new products. The couple accommodates everything their neighbors need. For this reason, local seniors come to the store for advice when something is bothering them. Young people come for help when they are in trouble. The couple even rewards young children who study hard. The entire community is like their family. It is a place filled with old-fashioned warmth.

Similarly, a general store owner in Miaoli also plants seeds of love in her community. She encourages everyone to do one good deed per day. In order to support the "Return to the Bamboo Bank Era" movement, she made a large bamboo bank more than one meter tall with three separate segments. She labeled $10 NT, $5 NT, and $1 NT on each segment to make it easier to sort coins.

Practicing what she preaches, every day she deposits the proceeds of her first sale into the bamboo bank, regardless of the amount. Her exemplary actions have influenced her neighbors in nearby streets. Every day they pass by the store and drop some coins into the bamboo bank, even if they do not make a purchase. The owner hopes that everyone in the community will be kind, do good deeds each day, and be happy to see each other. This is another heart-warming store that gives everyone the opportunity to accumulate virtue and goodwill.

A pure human touch means not only caring for oneself, but also for everyone in the community. For example, southern Taiwan was severely flooded after it was hit by Typhoon Morakot. Flood water also brought mudslides. In some areas the water level reached the top of the first floor. After the water receded, the first floors of many buildings were half-filled with mud. Many Tzu Chi volunteers lived in the disaster area and were victims themselves. Although they suffered tremendous losses as well, they were able to let go of their worries. They put on their blue-and-white uniforms and immediately joined other volunteers in relief efforts.

One Tzu Chi volunteer said, "Right now I am not a disaster victim. Rather, I am a Tzu Chi volunteer." Her home had been severely damaged, but instead of cleaning up her own house, she helped clean up her neighbors' houses. Moreover, she embraced and encouraged the victims by saying, "Don't be afraid. The disaster is over. Now we must be brave and upbeat, and return to our normal lives."

Such is the life-force of Taiwan.

● Inscribing a Touching Chapter in History

Many years ago, I talked with a famous author. He asked me, "What is the problem of modern society? Could you provide a brief answer?"

"Love-deficiency syndrome," I replied. A society that lacks love is like a body that lacks the ability to produce blood. Anemia and other diseases are bound to follow. How do we cure them? Only with love.

The Tzu Chi missions began with charity work. We had a common idea: love, pure and selfless great love. And we put that love into action. Otherwise, how can intangible love give practical help to those in need?

When the disaster in Myanmar first struck, the damage was

severe and the victims desperately needed relief aid. However, due to Myanmar's military rule, many compassionate people were unable to gain access to the country. With gratitude, respect, and love, Tzu Chi volunteers in neighboring Malaysia and Thailand entered the disaster areas. They joined forces with local kind-hearted people. Maintaining a low profile, they assessed the damage and learned the needs of the victims.

Tzu Chi volunteers responded in a timely manner to the pressing needs of the victims, and provided them with appropriate help. For example, the victims needed raincoats badly because it had been raining constantly and the temporary shelters were not completely covered. They also needed containers to hold drinking water. I saw Tzu Chi volunteers gently put raincoats on the children as if they were their parents. Their love and care as they distributed relief supplies deeply touched the locals. The government, having learned about Tzu Chi volunteers' work, sent an official letter to Tzu Chi granting full passage to the country. Thus, Tzu Chi had the opportunity to provide more assistance in Myanmar.

A road paved with love becomes ever broader. After the flooding from Typhoon Morakot, kind-hearted people from all over Taiwan took action. They traveled to southern Taiwan to help with the clean up. A total of 150,000 volunteers showed up during that period of time. Each person contributed sincerely from the bottom of their hearts. Otherwise, how could they have cleaned up garbage and filth in the smelly, endless mud and mire? Tzu Chi dispatched many heavy-duty machines and various vehicles to the disaster areas. Tzu Chi volunteers purchased tools and boots at their own expense, so they were donating money as well as their time and energy.

Many companies and business owners also provided material supplies and manpower. The transportation industry offered free rides to take relief personnel to disaster areas. Because of the contribution of all these people, the disaster areas were able to quickly resume their normal operations. The power of love and the spirit of compassion are indeed touching chapters in human history.

Chapter 8 - Building a Vision of Beauty and Benevolence

Dr. Edgar Mitchell was the sixth astronaut to walk on the moon. He has said that looking from space, the earth is just a sphere. There are no boundaries between countries, racial differences, or disputes and wars. He meant that if we went to another planet and introduced ourselves to the beings there, we would not tell them that we came from the United States or some other country. We would simply say that we came from Earth.

From his words, we understand that we should open our hearts and keep our eyes on the whole world instead of limiting ourselves to a small scope. We all must coexist with the Earth. When the Earth is damaged and natural disasters are frequent, none will be spared.

 Section One – Coexist with the Earth

In 2004, a severe earthquake near Indonesia triggered a tsunami that affected twelve nations in South and Southeast Asia. A disaster anywhere is a warning for us to heighten our vigilance. We should never think that a disaster in another country has nothing to do with us. We live on the same Earth. Each of us in the world should expand our love to care for all sentient beings, and help all those who need help.

● Every Life is Equally Precious

The Buddha teaches us that all sentient beings, whether virtuous or foolish, are equal. Even young people and those without education all have inconceivable wisdom. Therefore, we should never underestimate anyone.

I read a news story online about a five-year-old child who grew up in a single-parent family. His mother had a deteriorating joint condition. When the mother was thirty, she had the bones of an eighty-year-old. As a result, she was unable to move around easily. When she dropped her walking cane on the floor, she was unable to bend down to pick it up. Even though her son was only ten months old and could not yet walk well, he would crawl to the cane and pick it up for his mother.

The boy gradually grew up. He started to walk and help his mother with household chores, such as sweeping the floor and wiping down tables and chairs. At age five, he had already learned how to cook and prepare meals for his mother. Later he even asked his mother to let him take volunteer training to learn how to care for patients.

In India, a ten-year-old boy saw many children begging on the street one day. "Why don't you go home?" he asked them.

One answered, "I have no mother or father."

Another said, "I have no home."

One even replied, "If I do not beg and go home empty-handed, I will be beaten."

He felt sorry for the children, so he began to write a screenplay. He directed the movie and acted in it. He wanted everyone to know about the daily life of the street kids, while at the same time encouraging and supporting them. Even though he was so young, he had the ability to show sympathy for others and carry out his ideas. We all have the same level of wisdom.

Many people are antagonistic towards one another because of differences in appearance. For example, some people consider their race superior to others. They regard other races as inferior and suppress them. As the population increases, the conflict grows even stronger, and clashes become frequent. We all have the Buddha's nature, but under the tow of karma we develop all kinds of afflictions. If we could return to the state of our pure nature where no difference exists between people, then we would have no discrimination in our minds.

In addition to treating everyone equally, animals have intelligent spirits and should also be treated with respect. I once met someone who raised a myna bird. When visitors entered the house, the bird would say, "Please take a seat. Have some tea." When the master's child rang the doorbell before entering the house, the bird would say, "So-and-so is home." It knows who is standing outside. In addition, the myna bird can calculate money as well as humans can.

I saw a news report about a nest of duck eggs found in an open field. Because the mother duck had disappeared, a group of wild chickens sat on the eggs until they hatched. If we could posses a love similar to the affection that these animals have, then that would be a true awakening.

Man is the master of all living beings. Other living beings cannot speak of their love or suffering. We should understand that every life is precious. How can we not love and care for all sentient beings and respect one another?

A poem tells us, "We are all brothers upon birth. Why limit this to blood relations?" We should open our hearts and expand our selfish small love into selfless great love.

● Open our Arms of Love

We are all one family living under the same sky and above the same earth. As long as each of us gives a bit of love, this love will accumulate into a strong force.

South Africa is vast. Although the country does not have many Tzu Chi volunteers, each volunteer has been working hard to spread the seeds of love. Take Mr. and Mrs. Fang in Ladysmith, for example. They hired a Zulu employee to work in their factory. This employee saw that Mr. and Mrs. Fang were kind-hearted, and that Tzu Chi volunteers contributed to the community by bringing peace and harmony wherever they went. The employee thought of his own village: it was poor, and the villagers often lost their tempers.

The employee told Mr. Fang about his village, hoping that Tzu Chi could go and help. Tzu Chi volunteers responded to the request and visited that village. At first, many locals were skeptical about Tzu Chi's intentions. No outsider ever visited the village, why did Tzu Chi volunteers dare to come? With genuine love, they had used their wisdom to bring forth courage and determination.

Tzu Chi volunteers not only distributed daily necessities to the villagers, they also established job training centers to teach them skills to make a living. They also helped the locals till a vegetable garden for the community and showed them how to grow vegetables.

After planting the seeds of love, the volunteers worked hard to nurture those seeds so that they would bear fruits of love. Now, there are already more than sixty local volunteers in the village. The job training centers have played a major role in allowing the locals to learn useful skills.

Mrs. Mita was a villager in her sixties. She and her husband raised three sons and one daughter, all of whom have married.

Unfortunately, the eldest son and daughter-in-law passed away, leaving behind a little girl. Mr. & Mrs. Mita took good care of the little girl, who always behaved well.

Seeing how Tzu Chi volunteers loved and cared for the villagers, Mrs. Mita was deeply moved. She witnessed Tzu Chi volunteers not only giving supplies to the villagers, but also teaching them how to take care of their fellow villagers. Mr. & Mrs. Mita both became Tzu Chi volunteers. Mr. Mita concentrated on taking care of the community vegetable garden and Mrs. Mita focused on caring for the villagers in need. She delivered meals, visited patients, and helped take care of young children.

After a while, their granddaughter became jealous. She felt that her grandparents only loved and cared for other people and left her to do all the household chores. She came to resent Tzu Chi. One day, Mrs. Mita fell ill. Many Tzu Chi volunteers came to care for her and keep her company. The girl was deeply moved. "These volunteers are from Taiwan," her grandmother told her, "They give us supplies and love. We must look after our own villagers and love them, too."

The granddaughter finally understood why her grandparents were so dedicated. In order to let them continue to help others, she took the initiative to do the household chores whenever she finished her schoolwork.

Love can cause changes to happen. After the tsunami in South and Southeast Asia, we built three Great Love Villages in Banda Aceh, Indonesia, for more than two thousand families. When we first decided to build these villages, local Tzu Chi volunteers said to me, "The local government advised us to build houses for victims, but not for the rebels."

I asked, "Did the rebels suffer damage?"

They replied, "Yes, they did."

I said, "Great love does not differentiate between victims. As long as they are victims, we should help them."

Upon completion of these Great Love Villages, there were scores of rebel families living in each village. Now that life was peaceful, they no longer felt anxious or worried. With a stable and peaceful life, they broke their ties with the rebel army. The streetlights in the village were not programmed to automatically turn off but, knowing that Tzu Chi promotes energy conservation, they took the initiative to patrol the streets and turn off streetlights when it was light. While patrolling the streets, they would also pick up recyclables.

Love can tame turbulent and unsettled minds. When we open our arms of love, blessings will come.

Section Two – A Stream that Purifies the World

What is a purifying stream? It is good words and good principles. If we can continuously spread good principles and speak good words, we will be able to purify people's minds. There are so many people, so many different mindsets in this world. If their minds are not as one, then the world, with all its different races, countries, and thoughts, will truly be complicated.

How can these minds all align in the same direction? If the right methods are applied, it is not difficult. Sometimes a simple good word is like a pure spring which can cleanse the filth within the heart. When good words enter the heart and are truly applied, it is good. Everyone's heart has a rich field within. In addition to carefully cultivating this field and sowing the seeds of love, we must frequently irrigate it, so that the seeds can sprout and grow into a Bodhi forest.

● A Purifying Stream from the Heart

In this world, everything requires a method. Farming requires its own method. Farmers must know the proper time to prepare the soil and plant seeds. Their plans must be in accordance with the laws of nature.

I often say, Dharma is like water. Nothing can survive without water. Water nourishes the myriad creatures, allowing them to grow and flourish. Water can also change the weather and keep the climate in balance. Therefore, the cycle of water is very important. Humans cannot live without water, either. When we have a cold, the doctor says, "Drink more water and get more rest." How can we maintain good health without water?

Life needs pure and clean water; wisdom-life also needs Dharma-water. We need education to learn the proper ethical codes of conduct and how to distinguish right from wrong, so that we do not forget our duties and responsibilities. However, we all make mistakes and commit wrongdoings, either intentionally or unintentionally. These mistakes create bad karma which do not disappear with time: the karmic seeds always exist. Therefore, we should sincerely repent for our wrongdoings and refrain from committing new wrongs.

Repentance means understanding our wrongdoings and steadfastly committing not to transgress again. We should cleanse the filth within our hearts with wisdom and patience. If we can repent, we can achieve purification.

Some say, "I know I should change, but it is very difficult." Actually, since habitual tendencies are influenced by our surrounding environment, if we live in a good and loving environment we will be positively influenced and become benevolent, even if we used to have bad habits. This is the cleansing power of a purifying stream. Therefore, it is a matter of choice. It all depends on whether we choose a bad environment or a good environment.

Miss Gao has had a good life. She used to think that she had much free time, so she indulged in playing mahjong. As a result, she not only wasted time but also damaged her health and her relationship with her family. Fortunately, she met some benefactors in her life and exercised her wisdom to make the right choices. She changed in time to lead a positive life.

Now Miss Gao is a Tzu Chi volunteer who is committed to doing good deeds. When she hears good words or good deeds, she earnestly writes them down in her notebook. She has already filled more than ten notebooks and she generously shares these good words with others. One day she passed beneath a bridge where taxi drivers congregated. She saw many taxi drivers gambling and drinking. She thought to herself that drinking could easily cause car accidents and would hurt the drivers and their families.

So Miss Gao used her wisdom to create opportunities for those drivers to learn about the Dharma. On the first and fifteenth of each month, she enlisted other Tzu Chi volunteers to cook delicious vegetarian food for the drivers. In the beginning, some of the drivers paid no attention to her. She gracefully accepted this cold treatment.

She and other Tzu Chi volunteers continued to do this. As time passed, the drivers were gradually moved by her actions. Miss Gao also installed a television set for them to watch Da Ai Television during their break time so that they could have the opportunity to connect with good people and good deeds. Now no one drinks and gambles in that spot. This is an example of a way to transform others, by using a good environment to positively influence and transform people.

There are many ethnic Chinese people in Malaysia. The government sponsors community activities every year and invites many non-governmental organizations to participate. In recent years, the government has taken notice of Tzu Chi's humanistic culture and believes it is very good. So the government often invites Tzu Chi to take part in these community activities. Once, during Chinese New Year, the government sponsored a theme of Chinese festivals and asked Tzu Chi to run an exhibit on the Tomb Sweeping Festival. Due to local religious taboos, local Chinese avoid mentioning the words "death" or "tomb," especially during the Chinese New Year. With these restrictions, it was quite a challenge to exhibit the Tomb Sweeping Festival and the traditional custom of paying respect to one's ancestors.

The local Tzu Chi volunteers used their creativity to illustrate the beauty of human nature without breaking these taboos. They took this opportunity to explain the essence of the Tomb Sweeping Festival, which is showing gratitude and reverence to ancestors, and encouraged people to be filial to family elders. They decorated a three-hundred-meter stretch of a city street to represent the path of filial piety and the path of benevolence, promoting the idea that Filial piety and good deeds should not be delayed.

This activity attracted many people. Children, teenagers, and adults all came to the event with their parents. On the site, visitors learned the etiquette of kneeling and serving tea to parents and elders. The program wholly demonstrated the humanistic culture of respecting elders and educating the younger generation. It encouraged everyone to pay attention to their filial duties and not shy away from expressing filial piety.

The path of benevolence was arranged to exhibit the Bamboo Bank Era. The exhibit helped visitors become aware that the world is full of sufferings, and that many poverty-stricken people need urgent help. It encouraged everyone to discipline themselves, to do good deeds, and to refrain from a lavish and wasteful lifestyle. Many bamboo banks were available for visitors to adopt, conveying the message that everyone's love can accumulate into a powerful force.

In Malaysia, there is also a large population of Malays who do not understand Chinese. Islam is the major religion, but there are many other religious groups as well. With lively activities, Tzu Chi volunteers drew in crowds of mixed races and religions. Most importantly, they focused on the humanitarian spirit. They also successfully illustrated traditional Chinese culture with modern examples. The exhibit was truly a purifying stream that went deep into everyone's heart.

● Do Good to Create A Pure Land

A few years ago someone asked me, "If Tzu Chi volunteers have been doing such a great job recycling, why do we still see garbage everywhere?"

I replied, "We can look at this problem from a different angle. We are lucky to have recycling volunteers picking up such a multitude of reusable material and reducing the amount of trash. Otherwise, there would be even more garbage in the streets."

We should handle every matter with this same attitude. We need not complain, but should rather change our own mindset. If everyone becomes conscious of recycling and does not want to see streets littered with garbage, if everyone can focus on picking up the paper or plastic bottles beneath our feet, our environment will be clean and beautiful.

The cities of Luoshui and Hanwang were severely damaged in the 2008 Sichuan earthquake. Tzu Chi volunteers went to the disaster area to care for and comfort the survivors. They also encouraged locals to work with them to care for their fellow villagers. As a result, the locals are now able to both look after those in need and love their environment. Many locals also became recycling volunteers. Because they do recycling work, these volunteers noticed the tremendous amount of garbage and came to realize that natural resources are being depleted at an alarming rate. Therefore, they now understand the importance of conserving energy, reducing carbon emissions and cherishing materials.

One local mother indulged in gambling. Whenever she gambled, she lost track of day and night. She neglected all housework, was ill-tempered with her family when she lost, and even took up smoking and drinking. Her daughter felt neglected, so she envied other families. Later, persuaded by Tzu Chi volunteers, the mother decided to rid herself of her bad habits. She became a Tzu Chi volunteer and devoted her time to meaningful activities. She constantly reminded herself to fulfill her duties and take good care of her family. This change brought warmth back to her family, and made her daughter very happy.

After the earthquake, we helped build thirteen schools in Sichuan. During construction, Tzu Chi volunteers often came to care for the construction workers. In order to provide the students with a good learning environment, the workers gave up their eight-day Mid-Autumn Festival holiday and continued construction work. Furthermore, when Southern Taiwan was severely damaged by floods in 2009, the workers and the construction supervisors all donated money to help the flood victims. Local students also took the initiative to raise funds. This cycle of love is a purifying stream.

The purifying stream can cleanse the heart. One more living Bodhisattva means one less dysfunctional family. When each family in the community is kind and neighborly to other families, the community will be safe and peaceful. When numerous such communities are united, a harmonious society is formed. Therefore, each individual is important: with a pure heart, everyone can benefit humankind. Once we all have the same pure heart, our Earth will be a Pure Land.